T0214771

Practical Python Data Visualization

A Fast Track Approach To Learning Data Visualization With Python

Ashwin Pajankar

Apress®

Practical Python Data Visualization: A Fast Track Approach To Learning Data Visualization With Python

Ashwin Pajankar
Nashik, Maharashtra, India

ISBN-13 (pbk): 978-1-4842-6454-6   ISBN-13 (electronic): 978-1-4842-6455-3
https://doi.org/10.1007/978-1-4842-6455-3

Copyright © 2021 by Ashwin Pajankar

Managing Director, Apress Media LLC: Welmoed Spahr
Acquisitions Editor: Aditee Mirashi
Development Editor: James Markham
Coordinating Editor: Aditee Mirashi

Cover designed by eStudioCalamar

Cover image designed by Freepik (www.freepik.com)

Distributed to the book trade worldwide by Springer Science+Business Media 1 New York Plaza, New York, NY 10004. Phone 1-800-SPRINGER, fax (201) 348-4505, e-mail orders-ny@springer-sbm.com, or visit www.springeronline.com. Apress Media, LLC is a California LLC and the sole member (owner) is Springer Science + Business Media Finance Inc (SSBM Finance Inc). SSBM Finance Inc is a **Delaware** corporation.

For information on translations, please e-mail booktranslations@springernature.com; for reprint, paperback, or audio rights, please e-mail bookpermissions@springernature.com.

Apress titles may be purchased in bulk for academic, corporate, or promotional use. eBook versions and licenses are also available for most titles. For more information, reference our Print and eBook Bulk Sales web page at http://www.apress.com/bulk-sales.

Any source code or other supplementary material referenced by the author in this book is available to readers on GitHub via the book's product page, located at www.apress.com/978-1-4842-6454-6. For more detailed information, please visit http://www.apress.com/source-code.

Printed on acid-free paper

I dedicate this book to Abhijit Banerjee, Nobel Laureate economist of Indian origin

Table of Contents

About the Author

Ashwin Pajankar holds a Master of Technology from IIIT Hyderabad, and he has more than 25 years of programming experience. He started his journey in programming and electronics at the tender age of seven with the BASIC programming language and is now proficient in Assembly programming, C, C++, Java, Shell scripting, and Python. His other technical experience includes single-board computers such as Raspberry Pi and Banana Pro, and Arduino. He is currently a freelance online instructor teaching programming bootcamps to more than 60,000 students from tech companies and colleges. His YouTube channel has an audience of 10,000 subscribers and he has published more than 15 books on programming and electronics with many additional international publications.

About the Technical Reviewers

Lentin Joseph is an author, roboticist, and robotics entrepreneur from India. He runs robotics software company Qbotics Labs in Kochi and Kerala. He has ten years of experience in the robotics domain, primarily in Robot Operating System (ROS), OpenCV, and PCL. He has authored eight books on ROS, including *Learning Robotics Using Python, Mastering ROS for Robotics Programming, ROS Robotics Projects,* and *Robot Operating System for Absolute Beginners. He* has pursued his master's degress in robotics and automation in India and also worked at the Robotics Institute at Carnegie Mellon University. He has also been a TEDx speaker.

Aarthi Elumalai is a programmer, educator, entrepreneur, and innovator. She has a Bachelor of Engineering degree in computer science from Anna University, Chennai, India. She has launched a dozen web apps, plug-ins, and software applications that are being used by thousands of customers online. She has more than 15 years of experience in programming. She is the founder of DigiFisk, an e-learning platform that has more than 70,000 students worldwide.

Her courses are well-received by the masses, and her unique, project-based approach is a refreshing change for many. She teaches the complex world of programming by using practical exercises and puzzles along the way. Her courses and books always come with hands-on training in creating real-world projects so her students are better equipped for the real world.

Acknowledgments

I want to express my gratitude to all of the technical reviewers for helping me to make this book better. I would also like to express my gratitude to the team from Apress. Aditee Mirashi helped us to coordinate the entire book process. I am also grateful to Celestin Suresh for giving me the opportunity to write this book.

Introduction

I have been working with the Python programming language for more than 15 years now. I have used it for a variety of tasks like automation, graphics, Internet of Things (IoT), and data science. I have found that it is a very good tool for generating scientific and data-driven business visualizations. It takes fewer lines of code to generate visualizations with Python. Python is capable of fetching data from various type of sources. Combining this feature with various third-party visualization libraries makes Python the perfect tool for various types of visualization requirements.

This book covers the basics of Python, including setup and various modes, and many visualization libraries. I have also made a modest attempt to visualize real-life data related to the ongoing COVID-19 pandemic.

I encourage readers to read all of the material and not to skip anything, even if you are familiar with the particular topic. I have written this book in such a way that every topic and demonstration builds confidence in the reader for the next topic. This truly is a step-by-step guide for beginners and experts alike.

After reading this book, you will be empowered by the knowledge of data visualization with Python and will be able to apply this knowledge in real-life projects at your workplace. It will also instill confidence in you to explore more libraries for data visualization in Python, as most of the support the scientific Python ecosystem and NumPy library discussed in detail in this book.

I hope that readers of this book will enjoy reading it and following the demonstrations as much as I enjoyed writing it.

CHAPTER 1

Introduction to Python

I welcome you all to the exciting journey of learning data visualization with Python 3. This chapter provides details to get you started with the Python programming language, including its history, features, and applications. This chapter is focused on general information about Python 3 and its installation on various popular operating system (OS) platforms, such as Microsoft Windows, Ubuntu, and Raspberry Pi Raspbian. We will be writing a few basic Python programs and learn how to execute them on various platforms. Here is the list of topics that we will cover in this chapter.

- Python programming language
- Installing Python on various platforms
- Python modes

After completing this chapter, you should be comfortable with installation and usage of Python 3 programming language in various modes.

Python Programming Language

Python 3 is a high-level, interpreted, general-purpose programming language. This section provides a general discussion about the Python programming language and its philosophy.

© Ashwin Pajankar 2021
A. Pajankar, *Practical Python Data Visualization*,
https://doi.org/10.1007/978-1-4842-6455-3_1

History of Python

Python is a successor to the **ABC** programming language, which itself was inspired by the **ALGOL 68** and **SETL** programming languages. It was created by **Guido Van Rossum** as a personal side project during vacations in the late 1980s while he was working at CWI Centrum Wiskunde & Informatica in the Netherlands. From the initial release of Python through July 2018, Van Rossum was the lead developer and Benevolent Dictator for Life for this project. Since then, he has gone into a state of permanent vacation and now works on a steering committee for Python. The following timeline details the important milestones in Python's release.

- February 1991: Van Rossum published the code (labeled version 0.9.0) to alt.sources.

- January 1994: Version 1.0 was released.

- October 2000: Python 2.0 was released.

- December 2006: Python 3.0 was released.

- December 2019: Python 2.x was officially retired and is no longer supported by the Python Software Foundation.

Python 2.x versions are retired and no longer supported. In addition, Python 3 is not backward compatible with Python 2. Python 3 is the latest and currently supported version the language. We therefore use Python 3 throughout the book to demonstrate programs for data visualization. Unless explicitly mentioned, Python denotes Python 3 throughout this book.

Python Enhancement Proposals

To steer the development, maintenance, and support of Python, the Python leadership team came up with the concept of Python Enhancement Proposals (PEPs). These are the primary mechanism for suggesting new features and fixing issues in Python project. You can read more about the PEPs at the following URLs:

- `https://www.python.org/dev/peps/`

- `https://www.python.org/dev/peps/pep-0001/`

Philosophy of Python

The philosophy of Python is detailed in PEP20, known as **The Zen of Python,** available at `https://www.python.org/dev/peps/pep-0020/`. Here are some of the points from that PEP.

1. Beautiful is better than ugly.

2. Explicit is better than implicit.

3. Simple is better than complex.

4. Complex is better than complicated.

5. Flat is better than nested.

6. Sparse is better than dense.

7. Readability counts.

8. Special cases aren't special enough to break the rules.

9. Although practicality beats purity.

10. Errors should never pass silently.

11. Unless explicitly silenced.

12. In the face of ambiguity, refuse the temptation to guess.

13. There should be one—and preferably only one—obvious way to do it.

14. Although that way may not be obvious at first unless you're Dutch.

15. Now is better than never.

16. Although never is often better than *right* now.

17. If the implementation is hard to explain, it's a bad idea.

18. If the implementation is easy to explain, it may be a good idea.

19. Namespaces are one honking great idea—let's do more of those!

These are among the general philosophical guidelines that influenced the development of the Python programming language and continue to do so.

Applications of Python

Because Python is a general-purpose programming language, it has numerous applications in the following areas:

1. Web development.

2. Graphical user interface (GUI) development.

3. Scientific and numerical computing.

4. Software development.

5. System administration.

Case studies of Python for various projects are available at https://www.python.org/success-stories/.

Installing Python on Various Platforms

A Python implementation is a program or an environment that supports the execution of programs written in Python. The original implementation created by Van Rossum is known as CPython and serves as a reference implementation. Throughout the book, we use CPython. It is available on the Python website and we will learn how to install it in this section.

I prefer to write Python programs on a Windows computer or a Raspberry Pi computer with Raspberry Pi OS. Let us learn how to install Python on both of these platforms.

Installing on a Windows Computer

Visit the Python 3 download page located at `https://www.python.org/downloads/` and download the Python 3 setup file for your computer. It will automatically detect the OS on your computer and show the appropriate downloadable file, as displayed in Figure 1-1.

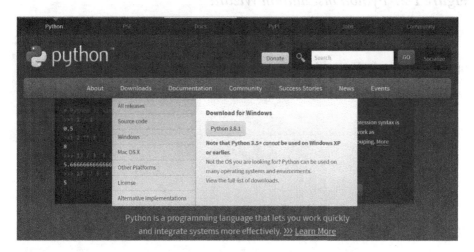

Figure 1-1. *Python Project home page with download options*

Run the setup file to install Python 3. During installation, select the check box related to adding Python 3 to the PATH variable (Figure 1-2).

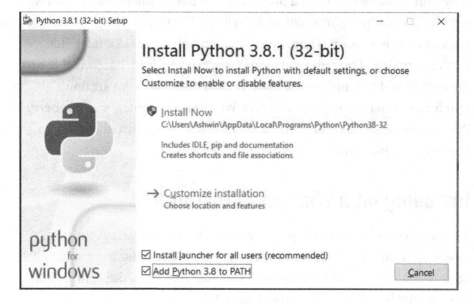

Figure 1-2. *Python Installation Wizard*

Click Customize Installation, which provides the customization options shown in Figure 1-3.

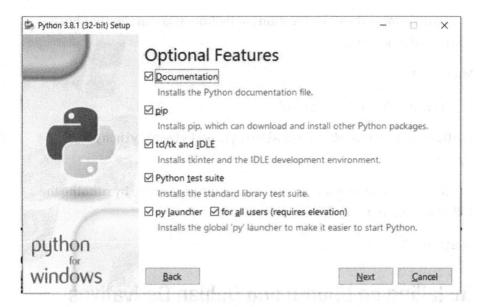

Figure 1-3. *Python installation options*

Select all the check boxes and click Next to continue the setup.
Complete the setup. The name of the binary executable program for
Python is python on Windows OS. Once installation is finished, run the
following command at the Windows command prompt cmd.

```
python -V
```

It will return the version of Python 3 as follows:

```
Python 3.8.1
```

We can also check the version of pip3 as follows:

```
pip3 -V
```

pip stands for Pip installs Python or Pip installs Packages; its name is
a recursive acronym. It is a package manager for the Python programming
language. We can install the other needed Python libraries for our
demonstrations using the pip utility.

To determine the exact locations of Python, you can run the where command as follows:

```
where python
```

It returns the following result:

```
C:\Users\Ashwin\AppData\Local\Programs\Python\Python38-32\
python.exe
```

Similarly, we can learn the location of the pip3 utility by running the following command:

```
where pip3
```

Installing on Ubuntu and Debian Derivatives

Debian is a popular distribution. Ubuntu Linux and Raspberry Pi OS are other popular distributions based on Debian. Python 3 and pip3 come preinstalled on all the Debian distributions and derivatives like Ubuntu or Raspberry Pi OS, so we do not have to install them separately. I use Raspberry Pi OS on a Raspberry Pi 4B with 4 GB RAM. Both the major Python versions, Python 2 and Python 3, come preinstalled on Debian derivatives. Their executables are named python and python3 for Python 2 and Python 3, respectively. We must use python3 for our demonstrations. To determine the versions and locations of the needed binary executable files, run the following commands one by one.

```
python3 -V
pip3 -V
which python3
which pip3
```

Almost all the other popular Linux distributions come with Python preinstalled, too.

Python Modes

Python has various modes that we will discuss one by one. First, though, we need to learn about the integrated development and learning environment (IDLE). This is an integrated development environment (IDE) developed by the Python Software Foundation for Python programming. When we install the CPython implementation of Python 3 on Windows, IDLE is also installed. We can launch it on the Windows OS in various ways. The first way is to search for it in the Windows Search bar by typing IDLE as shown in Figure 1-4.

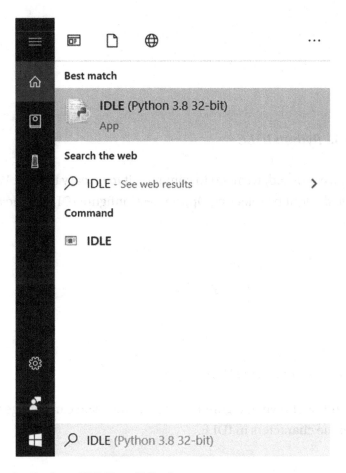

Figure 1-4. *Python IDLE on Windows*

The other way is to launch it from the command prompt (cmd) by running the following command:

```
idle
```

This will launch the window shown in Figure 1-5.

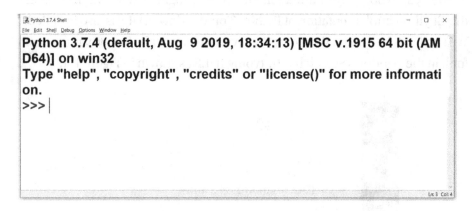

Figure 1-5. *Python IDLE*

Before we proceed, we need to configure it to be easy to read. We can change the font by selecting Options ➤ Configure IDLE as shown in Figure 1-6.

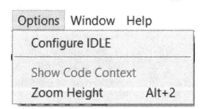

Figure 1-6. *Configuring IDLE*

The window shown in Figure 1-7 opens. There you can change the font and size of the characters in IDLE.

Figure 1-7. *IDLE configuration*

Adjust the font settings according to your own preferences.

All the Linux distributions might not come with IDLE preinstalled. We can install it on Debian and its derivatives (Ubuntu and Raspberry Pi OS) by running the following commands in sequence.

```
sudo apt-get update
sudo apt-get install idle3
```

Once the installation is complete, we can find IDLE on the menu (in this case the Raspberry Pi OS menu) as shown in Figure 1-8.

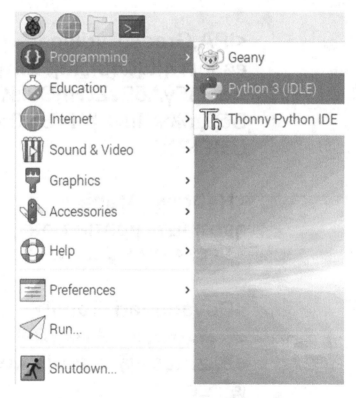

Figure 1-8. *IDLE on the Raspberry Pi OS menu*

We can also launch IDLE on Linux by running the following command:

```
idle
```

Now let us discuss the various Python modes.

Interactive Mode

Python's interactive mode is a command-line type of shell that executes the current statement and gives immediate feedback in the console. It runs the previously fed statements in active memory. As new statements are fed into and executed by the interpreter, the code is evaluated. When we open IDLE, we see a command-line prompt that is Python's interactive mode. Let's look at a simple example. Let's type in the customary Hello World program in the interactive prompt as follows:

```
print('Hello World!')
```

Press Enter to feed the line to the interpreter and execute it. Figure 1-9 presents a screenshot of the output.

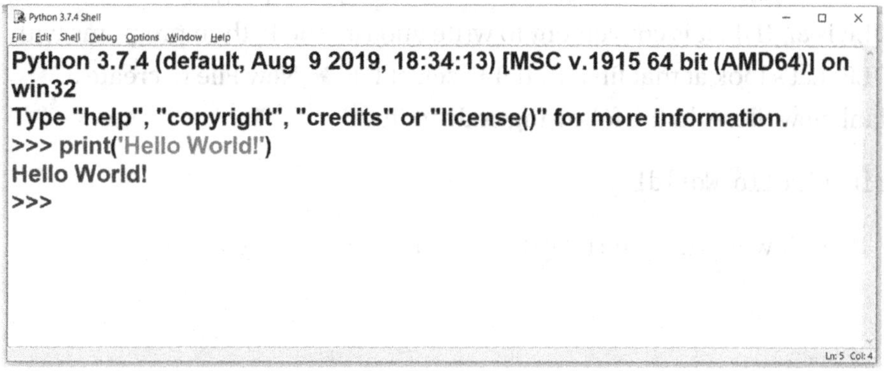

Figure 1-9. Python interactive mode on IDLE

We can launch Python interactive mode from the command prompt, too. At the Linux command prompt (e.g., lxterminal), we must run the command python3 and at the Windows command prompt cmd, we have to run the command python to launch it. Figure 1-10 is a screenshot of the interactive mode at the Windows command prompt.

```
C:\Users\Ashwin>python
Python 3.8.3 (tags/v3.8.3:6f8c832, May 13 2020, 22:20:19) [MSC
v.1925 32 bit (Intel)] on win32
Type "help", "copyright", "credits" or "license" for more infor
mation.
>>>
```

Figure 1-10. *Python interactive mode at the Windows command prompt*

Script Mode

We can write a Python program and save it to disk. Then we can launch it in multiple ways. This is known as script mode. Let us demonstrate it in IDLE. We can use any text editor to write the Python program, but because IDLE is an IDE, it is convenient to write and run the Python programs with IDLE. Let's look at that first. In IDLE, select File ➤ New File to create a blank new file. Add the following code to that:

```
print('Hello World!')
```

Save it with the name prog01.py on the disk (Figure 1-11).

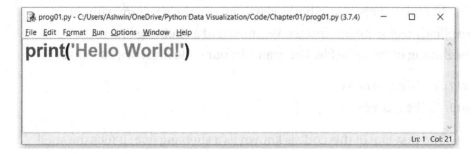

Figure 1-11. *A Python program in the IDLE code editor*

On the menu, click Run ➤ Run Module. This executes the program at the IDLE's prompt, as shown in Figure 1-12.

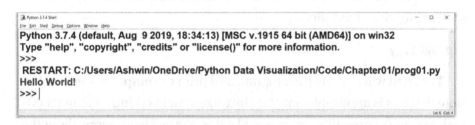

Figure 1-12. *A Python program under execution at the IDLE prompt*

We can even launch the program with Python's interpreter at the command prompt of the OS, too. Open the command prompt of the OS and navigate to the directory where the program is stored. At the Windows command prompt, run the following command:

```
python prog01.py
```

On the Linux terminal, we must run the following command prompt:

```
python3 prog01.py
```

Then the interpreter will run the program at the command prompt and the output (if any) will appear there.

15

In Linux, there is another way we can run the program without explicitly using the interpreter. We must add a **shebang** line to the beginning of the code file. For example, our code file looks like this:

```
#!/usr/bin/python3
print('Hello World!')
```

The first line of this code is known as a shebang line. It tells the shell what interpreter to use and its location. Run the following command to change the file permission to make it executable for the owner as follows:

```
chmod 755 prog01.py
```

Then we can directly launch our Python program file like any other executable with ./ as follows:

```
./prog01.py
```

The shell will execute the program and print the output to the terminal. Note that this is applicable only for Unix-like systems (Linux and macOS) as they support executing programs like this. We will learn more about the Python programming as and when we need from the next chapter onward.

Summary

This chapter started with the basics of the Python programming language. You learned how to write basic Python programs and execute them in various ways. You learned to work with Python on various OSs, including Windows and Linux. You also learned about various Python modes and how to launch them from the command prompts of various OSs.

In the next chapter, we will learn how to install Jupyter Notebook and take a brief tour of Jupyter Notebook.

CHAPTER 2

Exploring Jupyter Notebook

In Chapter 1, we acquainted ourselves with Python and learned how to write a very simple program with Python. We also saw how to use Python in both interactive mode and script mode. In this chapter, we explore Jupyter Notebook. In Chapter 1 we saw that interactive mode offers us the immediate feedback of Python statements. We will continue using the interactive mode of Python throughout the book almost all of the demonstrations. However, rather than using Python's built-in interactive mode with an interpreter, we will use another and much better tool known as the Jupyter tool. This entire chapter is dedicated to this topic.

You will learn about the following topics in this chapter:

- Overview of Jupyter Notebook.

- Setting up Jupyter Notebook.

- Running code in Jupyter Notebook.

After you complete this chapter, you should be comfortable with Python programming using Jupyter Notebook.

© Ashwin Pajankar 2021
A. Pajankar, *Practical Python Data Visualization*,
https://doi.org/10.1007/978-1-4842-6455-3_2

Overview of Jupyter Notebook

In Chapter 1, you learned various ways to run Python statements. We ran Python statements in a script and in the interpreter's interactive mode. The main advantage of using interactive mode is the immediate feedback. The main disadvantage of this mode is that, if we make any mistakes in typing the statements while and then execute the erroneous statement, we must rewrite the entire statement to reexecute it. It is also difficult to save it as a program. The option for saving the statements run on the interpreter can be found under the File menu option. However, all the statements and their outputs will be saved in plain text format with a .py extension. If there is any graphical output, it is displayed separately and cannot be stored along with the statements.

Owing to these limitations of interactive mode with interpreter, we will use a better tool for running the Python statements interactively in the web browser: Jupyter Notebook. Jupyter is a server program that can create interactive notebooks in a web browser.

A Jupyter notebook is a web-based notebook that is used for interactive programming with various languages, including Python, Octave, Julia, and R. It is very popular with people working in research domains. A Jupyter notebook can have code, visualizations, output, and rich text in a single file. The advantage of Jupyter Notebook over Python's own interactive prompt is that, users can edit the code and see the new output instantly, which is not possible in Python interactive mode. Another advantage is that we have the code, rich text elements, and the code's output (which could be in graphical or rich text format) in the same file on the disk. This makes it easy to distribute. We can save and share these notebooks over the Internet or using portable storage equipment. There are many services online that help us to store and execute Jupyter Notebook scripts on cloud servers.

Setting up Jupyter Notebook

We can easily install the Jupyter Notebook server program on any computer by running the following command at the command prompt:

```
pip3 install jupyter
```

Let's explore how we can use Jupyter Notebook for writing and executing Python statements. Run the following command at the OS command prompt to launch the Jupyter Notebook server process there:

```
jupyter notebook
```

Once the Jupyter notebook server process is launched, the command prompt window shows a server log, as displayed in Figure 2-1.

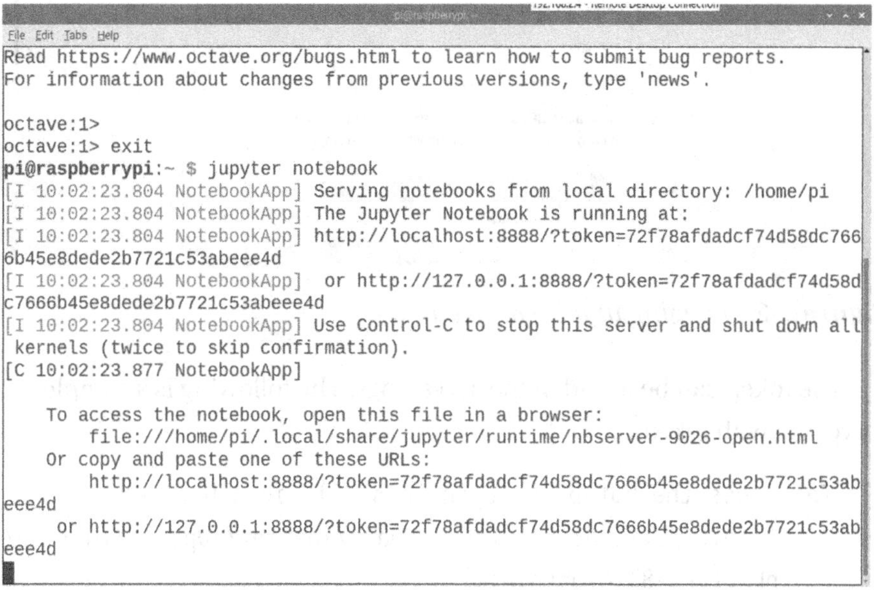

Figure 2-1. *Launching a new Jupyter Notebook process*

It launches a web page in the default browser in the OS. If the browser window is already open, it launches the page on a new tab of the same browser window. Another way to open the page (in case you accidentally close this browser window) is to visit `http://localhost:8888/` in your browser, which displays a page similar to the one shown in Figure 2-2.

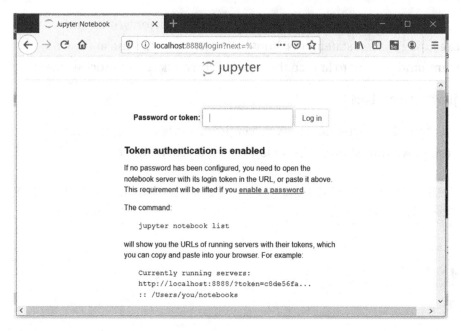

Figure 2-2. *Logging in with a token*

The token can be found in the server logs. The following is a sample server log with tokens.

```
To access the notebook, open this file in a browser:
    file:///C:/Users/Ashwin/AppData/Roaming/jupyter/runtime/
    nbserver-8420-open.html
Or copy and paste one of these URLs:
    http://localhost:8888/?token=e4a4fab0d8c22cd01b6530d5da
    ced19d32d7e0c3a56f925c
```

or http://127.0.0.1:8888/?token=e4a4fab0d8c22cd01b6530d5da
ced19d32d7e0c3a56f925c

In this log, we can see a couple of URLs. They refer to the same page (localhost and 127.0.0.1 are the same hosts). We can either copy and paste any of these URLs directly in the address bar of the browser tab and open the Jupyter Notebook home page or we can visit http://localhost:8888/ as previously mentioned and then paste the token in the server log (in our case it is e4a4fab0d8c22cd01b6530d5daced19d32d7e0c3a56f925c) and log in, which will take us to the same home page.

Note that every instance of the Jupyter Notebook server will have its own token and the token here will not work with your Jupyter Notebook. The token is only valid for that server process.

After you follow any one of the routes just explained, you will see a home page tab in the browser window that looks like Figure 2-3.

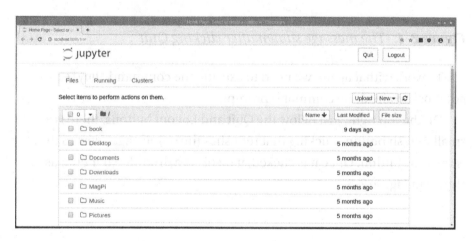

Figure 2-3. *A new home page tab of Jupyter Notebook*

You can see that there are three tabs on the web page itself: Files, Running, and Clusters. The Files tab shows the directories and files in the directory from where we launched the notebook server at the command prompt. In this example, I have executed the command jupyter notebook

from lxterminal of my Raspberry Pi. The present working directory is the
home directory of the pi user /home/pi. That is why we can see all the files
and directories in the home directory of my RPi computer in the screenshot
in Figure 2-3.

In the top right corner, there are Quit and Logout buttons. If you click
the Logout button, it logs out from the current session. To log in again,
you will again need the token or URL with the embedded token from the
notebook server log as discussed earlier. If you click Quit, that stops the
notebook server process running at the command prompt and displays the
modal message box shown in Figure 2-4.

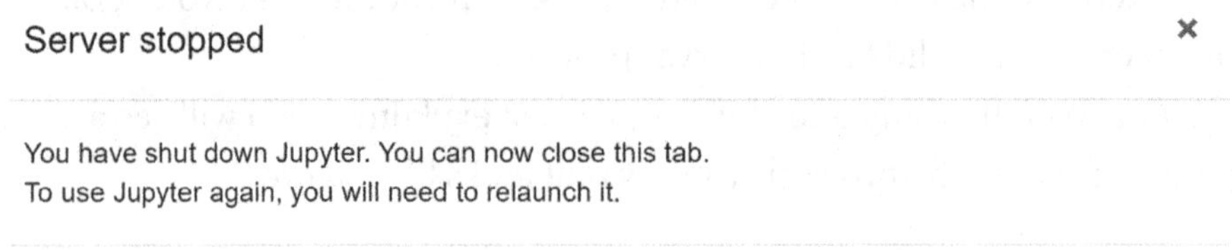

Server stopped   ✕

You have shut down Jupyter. You can now close this tab.
To use Jupyter again, you will need to relaunch it.

Figure 2-4. *The message shown after clicking Quit*

To work with it again, we need to execute the command jupyter
notebook again at the command prompt.

On the top right, just below the Quit and Logout buttons, there is a
small refresh button. Clicking that refreshes the home page. Next to that
is the New button. Once it is clicked, it displays a drop-down menu, as
shown in Figure 2-5.

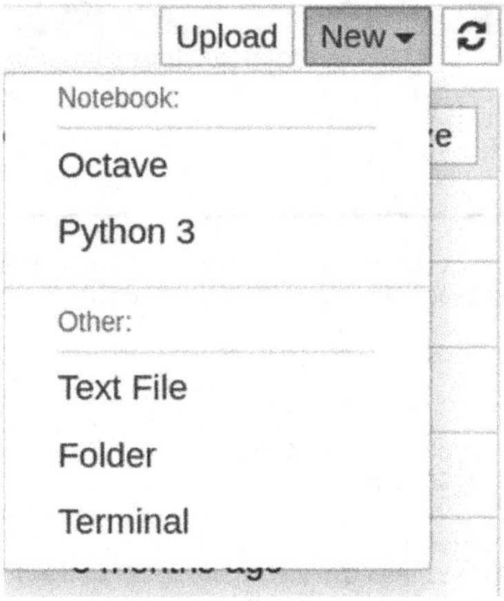

Figure 2-5. *Options for a new notebook*

As you can see, the drop-down menu is divided into two sections, Notebook and Other. In this example, you can choose to create Octave and Python 3 notebooks. If your computer has more programming languages installed that are supported by Jupyter Notebook, those additional languages will be displayed here as well. We can also create text files and folders. We can open a command prompt in the web browser by clicking Terminal. Figure 2-6 is a screenshot of lxterminal running in a separate web browser tab.

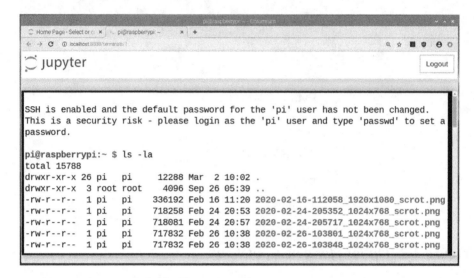

Figure 2-6. *A new lxterminal window within the browser*

Selecting Python 3 from the drop-down menu creates a new Python 3 notebook as shown in Figure 2-7.

Figure 2-7. *A new Python 3 notebook*

If you return to the home page by clicking the home page tab in the browser and then click the Running tab, you can see the entries corresponding to the terminal and the Python 3 notebook as shown in Figure 2-8.

Figure 2-8. *Summary of current Jupyter Notebook subprocesses*

Running Code in Jupyter Notebook

Go to the Python 3 Untitled1 tab again and type the following statement in the text area (also known as a cell):

```
printf("Hello, World!\n");
```

Click Run. Jupyter will execute that as a Python 3 statement and show the result immediately below the cell as shown in Figure 2-9.

Figure 2-9. *Code output in Jupyter Notebook*

As you can see, after execution, it automatically creates a new cell below the result and places the cursor there. Let's discuss the menu bar and the icons above the programming cells. We can save the file by clicking the floppy disk icon. We can add a new empty cell after the current cell by clicking the + icon. The next three icons are for cut, copy, and paste. Up and down arrows can shift the position of the current cell up and down, respectively. The next option is to run the cell, which we already saw. The next three icons are used to interrupt the kernel, restart the kernel, and restart the kernel and rerun all the cells in the notebook. Next to that, we have a drop-down menu that allows us to select what type of cell it should be. Figure 2-10 is a screenshot of the drop-down menu when clicked.

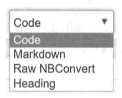

Figure 2-10. *Types of cells in Jupyter Notebook*

The cell is treated as a Python 3 code cell when you select the Code option. It is treated as a Markdown cell when you choose the Markdown option. Markdown is a markup language that can create rich text output. For example, anything followed by # creates a heading, anything followed by ## creates a subheading, and so on. Just type the following lines in a Markdown cell and execute it:

```
# Heading 1
## Heading 2
```

During our Python 3 demonstrations, we use the Markdown cells primarily for headings. However, you can further explore Markdown on your own. You can find more information about it at https:// jupyter-notebook.readthedocs.io/en/stable/examples/Notebook/

`Working%20With%20Markdown%20Cells.html`. The output of the preceding demonstration is shown in Figure 2-11.

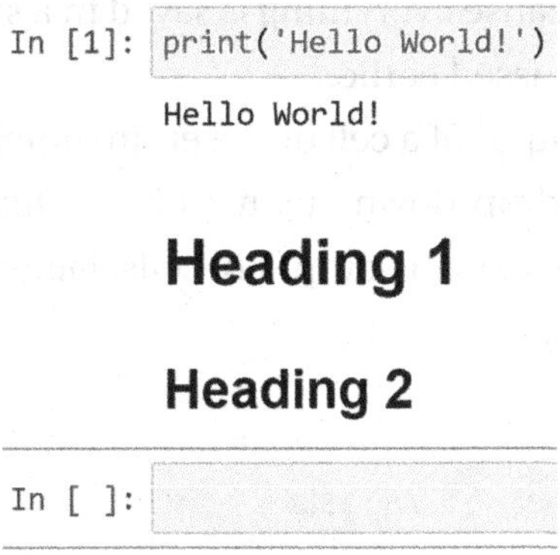

In [1]: `print('Hello World!')`

Hello World!

Heading 1

Heading 2

In [ ]:

Figure 2-11. *Headings in Markdown*

You can even change the name of the notebook file by clicking its name in the top part of the notebook. Once you click, it displays a modal box for renaming as shown in Figure 2-12.

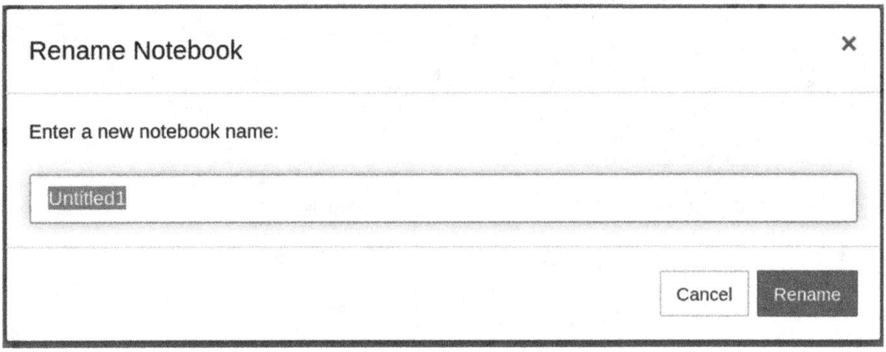

Rename Notebook   ✕

Enter a new notebook name:

Untitled1

Cancel   Rename

Figure 2-12. *Rename a notebook in Jupyter*

Rename it if you wish to do so. If we browse the location on disk from where we launched Jupyter Notebook at the command prompt, we will find the file with an `ipynb` extension, which stands for IPython Notebook.

In the same way, we can use Jupyter Notebook for interactive programming with the other programming languages that support Jupyter. We will mostly use this notebook format to store our code snippets for interactive sessions because everything is saved in a single file, which can be shared easily as discussed earlier.

We can clear the output of a cell or the entire notebook. On the menu bar, select Cell. On the drop-down menu, Current Outputs and All Output have Clear option that clears the output of cells. Figure 2-13 is a screenshot of the available options.

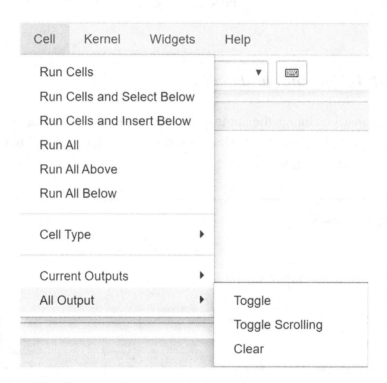

Figure 2-13. *Clearing the output in Jupyter*

One of the most significant advantages of Jupyter Notebook is that you can edit an already executed cell if there is any syntax error or you simply want to change the code. Jupyter Notebook is like an IDE that runs within a web browser and produces the output in the same window. This interactivity and the ability to keep code, rich text, and output in the same file has made Jupyter Notebook hugely popular worldwide. The kernel for running Python programs comes from the IPython project. As I mentioned earlier, we can use it for other programming languages, too. I have used it for running GNU Octave programs as well.

Note   You can find more information about Jupyter Notebook and IPython at the following URLs:

```
https://jupyter.org/
```

```
https://ipython.org/
```

Summary

In this chapter, we got started with installation of Jupyter Notebook on various platforms. We then explored how we can run simple Python statements in Jupyter Notebook. We learned that we can store the code and the output of that code in a single file that can be shared easily over the Internet.

In the next chapter, we will use Jupyter Notebook to work with simple visualizations using Python and a popular data visualization library, leather.

CHAPTER 3

Data Visualization with Leather

In Chapter 2, we acquainted ourselves with Python programming using Jupyter Notebook. You should now be comfortable writing interactive Python programs with Jupyter Notebook.

In this chapter, we will use Jupyter Notebook and Python with a data visualization library, leather, to produce basic visualizations. Here is the list of topics we will cover in this chapter:

- Introduction to leather
- More types of visualizations
- Scales
- Styling

Running OS Commands in Jupyter Notebook

You have seen how to use Jupyter notebook for Python programming. We will now explore how to execute an OS command in the notebook. This is useful, as we need to use pip to install many utilities and we can run it right from within the notebook.

© Ashwin Pajankar 2021
A. Pajankar, *Practical Python Data Visualization*,
https://doi.org/10.1007/978-1-4842-6455-3_3

Create a new Jupyter notebook for all the code in this chapter. We will follow this process for all of the chapters, so by the end of the book, we will have all the programs in notebooks by chapter.

To execute an OS command in a notebook cell, we have to use the **!** symbol as a prefix as follows:

```
!dir
```

The output of this command is shown in Figure 3-1.

```
In [4]:  !dir

         Volume in drive C has no label.
         Volume Serial Number is 9C4B-9156

         Directory of C:\Users\Ashwin\OneDrive\Python Data Visualization\Code\Chapter03

         06/21/2020  10:19 AM    <DIR>          .
         06/21/2020  10:19 AM    <DIR>          ..
         06/21/2020  10:13 AM    <DIR>          .ipynb_checkpoints
         06/21/2020  10:19 AM           75,464 Notebook1.ipynb
                        1 File(s)         75,464 bytes
                        3 Dir(s)  122,201,464,832 bytes free
```

Figure 3-1. *Output of an OS command in Jupyter Notebook*

You can upgrade the pip utility by running the following statement:

```
!pip3 install --upgrade pip
```

Install the library leather for data visualization demonstrations, using this statement:

```
!pip3 install leather
```

This installs the leather data visualization library on the computer. In the next section, we will get started with visualization with Python and leather using a notebook.

Introduction to Leather

Leather is an easy-to-use, popular data visualization library for Python. You can find this on the Python Package Index (PyPI) at https://pypi. org/project/leather/. PyPI is a repository of third-party packages that can be downloaded using the pip3 utility. We can also search for availability of a package on PyPI. Run the following command in the notebook:

```
!pip3 search leather
```

The output is shown in Figure 3-2.

```
In [5]:  !pip3 search leather
         leather (0.3.3)  - Python charting for 80% of humans.
            INSTALLED: 0.3.3 (latest)
         hearts (0.0.0)   - A simple charting library. Derived from https://github.com/w
         ireservice/leather.
```

Figure 3-2. *Searching for a package with pip3*

Before we can proceed further, we need to know a few things about the Python programming language in advance. In Python, tabs or indentations are used to denote code blocks. In a few popular programming languages like C, C++, and Java, multiline code blocks are enclosed in curly brackets {}. Python instead forces programmers to indent the code blocks and there is no other way to denote them. Consider the following code as an example.

```
a = 3
if a%2 == 0:
    print('Even')
else:
    print('Odd')
```

Run that code in the notebook and see the result. There is also a fun thing you can try. We have already learned about PEP 20, the Zen of Python. The Python creator added it as an Easter egg in the interpreter, and you can invoke it with the following statement:

```
import this
```

If you run the statement in the notebook, it prints all the statements in the Zen of Python in the output.

Note that whatever program we are going to demonstrate with Jupyter Notebook can also be run with the IDLE with a few changes. We are using Jupyter Notebook for its immediate feedback and interactive features. Now let's use the `import` statement to add the leather library to our notebook. We just need to import it once per session and it will be available to us throughout the session. Use this statement:

```
import leather
```

Run this and it imports the library to the current notebook session. It is a good idea to use a heading for every new topic, but I leave it to your discretion. You will find that I use headings quite often in the notebooks for the code bundle of this book to provide context and reference to whatever I am demonstrating. It is a good practice and you might want to follow it.

Let us write simple code for visualization of a few points. We can define the points in an X-Y coordinate system. We can use a list of tuples to define points as follows:

```
data1 = [(1.5, 2), (2, 3), (4.5, 6), (7.5, 4)]
```

We can also define them as a list of lists:

```
data1 = [[1.5, 2], [2, 3], [4.5, 6], [7.5, 4]]
```

We can also define them as a tuple of tuples:

```
data1 = ((1.5, 2), (2, 3), (4.5, 6), (7.5, 4))
```

We can also define them as a tuple of lists:

```
data1 = ([1.5, 2], [2, 3], [4.5, 6], [7.5, 4])
```

As you can see, the leather library is not very particular and is very flexible about how we define our data.

Let us define a chart object as follows:

```
chart = leather.Chart('Simple pairs of x-y')
```

Next, create a dot chart:

```
chart.add_dots(data1)
```

Then let's visualize the chart as follows:

```
chart.to_svg()
```

It will display the output in the same notebook, as shown in Figure 3-3.

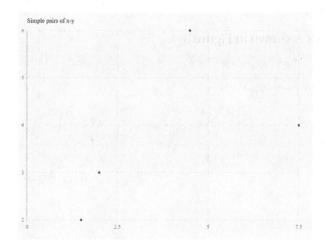

Figure 3-3. *Plotting the points*

We can save the image to disk with the following statement:

```
chart.to_svg('image1.svg')
```

We can then customize dots as follows:

```
chart = leather.Chart('Customised Dots')
chart.add_dots(data1, fill_color='#00ff00', radius=10)
chart.to_svg()
```

Let us define more data points:

```
data2 = [(2, 3), (4, 5), (5, 6), (7, 5)]
```

We can also visualize multiple series as follows:

```
chart = leather.Chart('Visualizing Multiple series')
chart.add_dots(data1)
chart.add_dots(data2)
chart.to_svg()
```

The output is shown in Figure 3-4.

Figure 3-4. *Plotting the multiple series*

As we can see in Figure 3-4, leather automatically assigns different colors to the points based on the series to which they belong.

More Types of Visualizations

We can visualize the data with line segments joining the points as follows:

```
chart = leather.Chart('Visualizing Lines')
chart.add_line(data1)
chart.to_svg()
```

The output is shown in Figure 3-5.

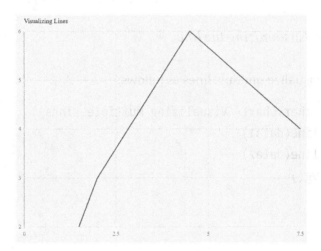

Figure 3-5. *Visualizations with line segments*

We can customize the line visualization as follows:

```
chart = leather.Chart('Customized Line')
chart.add_line(data1,stroke_color='#0000ff', width=3)
chart.to_svg()
```

Figure 3-6 displays the output.

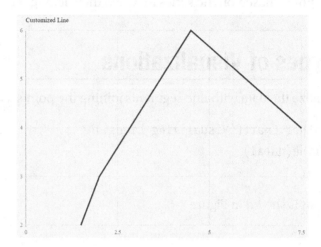

Figure 3-6. *Customizing the line*

We can visualize multiple lines as follows:

```
chart = leather.Chart('Visualizing Multiple Lines')
chart.add_line(data1)
chart.add_line(data2)
chart.to_svg()
```

Figure 3-7 shows the output.

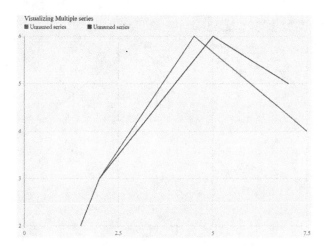

Figure 3-7. *Visualizing multiple lines*

We can visualize multiple types in a single visualization as follows:

```
chart = leather.Chart('Visualizing Multiple Types')
chart.add_line(data1)
chart.add_dots(data2)
chart.to_svg()
```

Figure 3-8 displays the output.

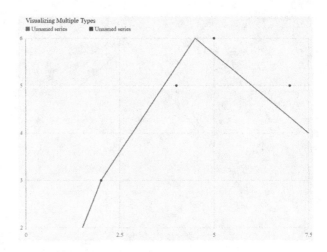

Figure 3-8. *Visualizing multiple types*

We can visualize with bars as follows:

```
data = [[1, 'A'], [2, 'B'], [3, 'C'], [4, 'D']]
chart = leather.Chart('Visualizing Bars')
chart.add_bars(data)
chart.to_svg()
```

In our data set, one of the dimensions is the text data. The visualization is shown in Figure 3-9.

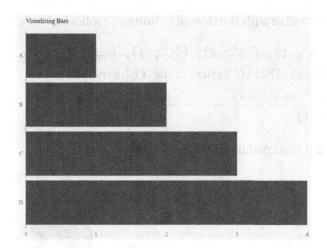

Figure 3-9. *Visualizing bar charts*

We can customize it as follows:

```
chart = leather.Chart('Customizing Bars')
chart.add_bars(data, fill_color='#777777')
chart.to_svg()
```

The output is displayed in Figure 3-10.

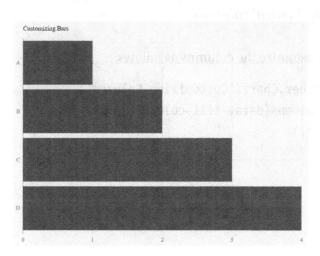

Figure 3-10. *Customizing bar charts*

We can visualize with horizontal columns as follows:

```
data = [ ('A', 1), ('B', 2), ('C', 3), ('D', 4)]
chart = leather.Chart('Visualizing Columns')
chart.add_columns(data)
chart.to_svg()
```

The output is shown in Figure 3-11.

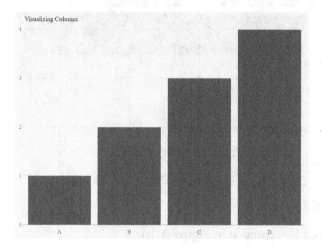

Figure 3-11. *Vertical columns*

We can customize the columns as follows:

```
chart = leather.Chart('Customizing Columns')
chart.add_columns(data, fill_color='#77ff77')
chart.to_svg()
```

The output is displayed in Figure 3-12.

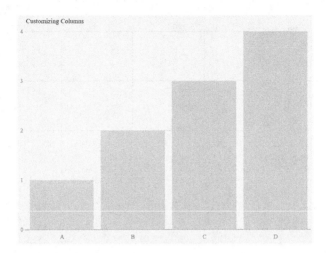

Figure 3-12. *Customizing vertical columns*

Scales

There are various types of scales the that leather library can create automatically and programmatically. An ordinal scale is automatically created for the text data. The example is the same as we saw earlier:

```
chart = leather.Chart('The Ordinal Scale')
chart.add_columns(data)
chart.to_svg()
```

Linear scales are created automatically when the data is numeric. We can set the limit of scales as follows:

```
chart = leather.Chart('Linear Scale')
chart.add_x_scale(1, 8)
chart.add_y_scale(1, 7)
chart.add_line(data1)
chart.to_svg()
```

Figure 3-13 displayes the output.

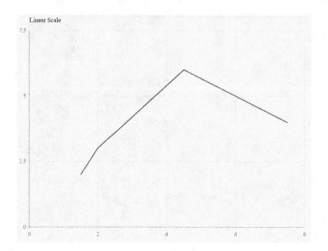

Figure 3-13. *Linear scale with custom limits*

A temporal scale is automatically created for temporal (time-related) data:

from datetime import date

```
data = [
    (date(2020, 1, 1), 4),
    (date(2020, 3, 1), 6),
    (date(2020, 6, 1), 2),
    (date(2020, 9, 1), 1)]

chart = leather.Chart('Temporal Scale')
chart.add_x_scale(date(2019, 9, 1), date(2020, 12, 1))
chart.add_line(data)
chart.to_svg()
```

The output is shown in Figure 3-14.

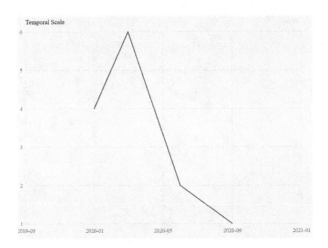

Figure 3-14. *Temporal scale with custom limits*

Styling

Leather provides a lot of styling options. We can set the tick values on the axes as per our requirements as follows:

```
chart = leather.Chart('Ticks Demo')
chart.add_x_scale(1, 8)
chart.add_x_axis(ticks=[1, 2, 3, 4, 5, 6, 7, 8])
chart.add_y_scale(1, 7)
chart.add_y_axis(ticks=[1, 2, 3, 4, 5, 6, 7])
chart.add_line(data1)
chart.to_svg()
```

The output is as shown in Figure 3-15.

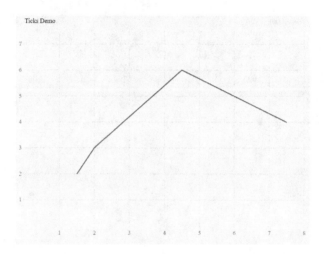

Figure 3-15. *Custom tick values*

We can also customize the font and colors used to show the values and the series in the visualization. The following is a simple example.

```
leather.theme.title_font_family = 'Times New Roman'
leather.theme.legend_font_family = 'Times New Roman'
leather.theme.tick_font_family = 'Times New Roman'
leather.theme.default_series_colors = ['#ff0000', '#00ff00']
chart = leather.Chart('Custom Fonts')
chart.add_line(data1)
chart.add_line(data2)
chart.to_svg()
```

Figure 3-16 shows the output for this example.

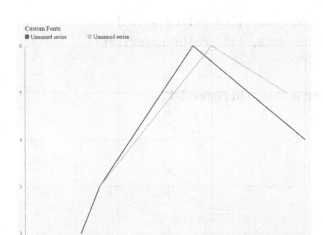

Figure 3-16. *Custom fonts and colors*

We can also color the data points according to their position with the following code. Let's import the random library into the notebook:

```
import random
```

We will use it to generate the data points as follows:

```
data = [(random.randint(0, 250),
         random.randint(0, 250)) for i in range(100)]
```

This creates 100 data points. The values of x and y axes for those 100 points are randomly chosen from the interval of 0 to 250. We can write a colorizer function that returns a color value in terms of RGB based on the location of the point.

```
def colorizer(location):
    return 'rgb(%i, %i, %i)' % (location.x, location.y, 150)
```

Let's call this function to define the fill color of the points as follows:

```
chart = leather.Chart('Colorized dots')
chart.add_dots(data, fill_color=colorizer)
chart.to_svg()
```

The output is shown in Figure 3-17.

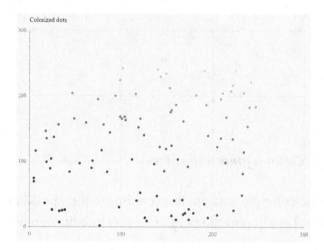

Figure 3-17. *Custom colors for data points*

Summary

This chapter introduced demonstrations of data visualization with Python using leather, a popular data visualization library. We saw different types of visualizations, styles, and scales. Leather is a very simple data visualization library and is capable of visualizing only simple shapes.

Your business requirements or scientific visualizations might necessitate more complex and elaborate visualizations. For that, you need to be comfortable with the scientific Python ecosystem. The next chapter explores the scientific Python ecosystem in detail. We will also learn the basics of NumPy n-dimensional arrays (also known as ndarrays).

CHAPTER 4

Scientific Python Ecosystem and NumPy

In Chapter 3, you learned how to create simple visualizations with Python 3 and the leather data visualization library. You also learned that only primitive visualizations can be prepared using the leather data visualization library. For more complex and elaborate visualizations, we need to use libraries with the advanced data handling and visualization capabilities.

This chapter explores the scientific Python ecosystem and its components. It also provides a brief overview of the NumPy library with a few coding demonstrations. The following topics are explored in this chapter:

- Scientific Python ecosystem

- NumPy and ndarrays

- Ndarray properties

- NumPy constants

Throughout the remaining chapters of this book, we will explore many components of the scientific Python ecosystem one by one. Throughout this book, we will be using different libraries that are part of this scientific Python ecosystem. The valuable knowledge you will gain in this chapter serves as foundation for the remaining chapters. As this is an introductory chapter for a broad ecosystem, I have kept it short, yet practical.

© Ashwin Pajankar 2021
A. Pajankar, *Practical Python Data Visualization*,
https://doi.org/10.1007/978-1-4842-6455-3_4

Scientific Python Ecosystem

The scientific Python ecosystem (SciPy) is a collection of Python libraries for mathematics, science, and engineering. SciPy has the following core components:

1. *Python programming languages:* We explored installation and a few basics of the Python 3 programming language in Chapter 1.

2. *NumPy:* This is the numerical Python library, the fundamental package for numerical computation in Python. It defines an *N*-dimensional data type that can be used for numerical computations on multidimensional data.

3. *SciPy library:* This includes many routines for mathematical and scientific computations that can be used for scientific applications.

4. *Matplotlib:* This is a MATLAB-inspired library for data visualization in Python 3.

There are several additional important member libraries of this ecosystem.

1. *Pandas:* This stands for Python data analysis. It provides versatile data structures such as series and data frame.

2. *SymPy:* This stands for symbolic Python. It is used for symbolic mathematics and algebra.

3. *scikit-image:* This library has routines for image processing.

4. *scikit-learn:* This library has routines for machine learning.

The interactive environments that are usually used with SciPy are IPython or Jupyter Notebook. We looked at Jupyter Notebook in detail in Chapter 2 and used it in Chapter 3 as well. We will continue using it for rest of this book.

The next section covers the NumPy library in greater detail.

NumPy and Ndarrays

As introduced earlier, NumPy is the fundamental package for numerical computation in Python. The most useful feature of the NumPy library is the multidimensional container data structure known as ndarray.

An ndarray is a multidimensional array (also known as a container) of items that have the same datatype and size. We can define the size and datatype of the items at the time of the creation of the ndarray. Just like the other data structures such as lists, we can access the contents of an ndarray with an index. The index in the ndarrays ranges from 0 (just like arrays in C or lists in Python). We can use ndarrays for a variety of computations. All the other libraries in SciPy and other libraries also recognize and use NumPy ndarrays and associated routines to represent their own data structures and operations on them.

Let's get started with a hands-on example. Create a new Jupyter notebook for this chapter, then run the following command to install the NumPy library:

```
!pip3 install numpy
```

Import it into the current notebook by running the following command:

```
import numpy as np
```

You can create a list and then use it to create a simple ndarray as follows:

```
l1 = [1, 2, 3]
x = np.array(l1, dtype=np.int16)
```

Here we are creating an ndarray from a list. The datatype of the members is 16-bit integer. You can find a detailed list of the datatypes supported at https://numpy.org/devdocs/user/basics.types.html.

We can write the preceding code in a single line as follows:

```
x = np.array(l1, dtype=np.int16)
```

Let's print the value of ndarray and its type (which, we know, is ndarray).

```
print(x)
print(type(x))
```

The output is as follows:

```
[1 2 3]
<class 'numpy.ndarray'>
```

As we can observe in the output, it is of the class numpy.ndarray. As we learned earlier, the indexing starts from 0. Let's demonstrate that by accessing the members of the ndarray as follows:

```
print(x[0]); print(x[1]); print(x[2])
```

Here is the output:

```
1
2
3
```

We can even use a negative index: -1 returns the last element, -2 returns the second to the last element, and so on. Here is an example:

```
print(x[-1])
```

If we provide any invalid index value, it throws an error.

```
print(x[3])
```

In this statement, we are trying to access the fourth element in the ndarray, which is nonexistent. It thus returns the following error:

```
IndexError                    Traceback (most recent call last)
<ipython-input-4-d3c02b9c2b5d> in <module>
----> 1 print(x[3])

IndexError: index 3 is out of bounds for axis 0 with size 3
```

More Than One Dimension

We can have more than one dimension for an array as follows:

```
x1 = np.array([[1, 2, 3], [4, 5, 6]], np.int16)
```

This represents a two-dimensional matrix with two rows and three columns. We can access individual elements as follows:

```
print(x1[0, 0]); print(x1[0, 1]); print(x1[0, 2]);
```

We can even access entire rows:

```
print(x1[0, :])
print(x1[1, :])
```

The output is shown here:

```
[1 2 3]
[4 5 6]
```

We can access an entire column with this syntax:

```
print(x[:, 0])
```

The output is as follows:

```
[1 4]
```

We can even have an ndarray with more than two dimensions. Here is the syntax to create a three-dimensional (3D) array:

```
x2 = np.array([[[1, 2, 3], [4, 5, 6]],[[0, -1, -2], [-3, -4,
-5]]], np.int16)
```

Scientific and business applications often use multidimensional data. Ndarrays are very useful for storing numerical data. Try to run the following items and retrieve the elements of the preceding 3D matrix.

```
print(x2 [0, 0, 0])
print(x2 [1, 1, 2])
print(x2[:, 1, 1])
```

Ndarray Properties

We can learn more about the ndarrays by referring to their properties. First, let's look at all the properties with the demonstration. This example uses the same 3D matrix we used earlier.

```
x2 = np.array([[[1, 2, 3], [4, 5, 6]],[[0, -1, -2], [-3, -4,
-5]]], np.int16)
```

We can learn the number of dimensions with the following statement:

```
print(x2.ndim)
```

The output returns the number of dimensions:

```
3
```

We can then learn the shape of the ndarray as follows:

```
print(x2.shape)
```

The shape indicates the size of the dimensions, as follows:

```
(2, 2, 3)
```

We can determine the datatype of the members as follows:

```
print(x2.dtype)
```

Here is the output:

```
int16
```

We can also learn the size (number of elements) and the number of bytes required in memory for storage as follows:

```
print(x2.size)
print(x2.nbytes)
```

The output is as follows:

```
12
24
```

We can compute the transpose with the following code:

```
print(x2.T)
```

NumPy Constants

The NumPy library has many useful mathematical and scientific constants you can use in your programs. The following code snippet prints all of those important constants:

```
print(np.inf)
```

```
print(np.NAN)
print(np.NINF)
print(np.NZERO)
print(np.PZERO)
print(np.e)
print(np.euler_gamma)
print(np.pi)
```

The output is as follows:

```
inf
nan
-inf
-0.0
0.0
2.718281828459045
0.5772156649015329
3.141592653589793
```

Summary

This chapter introduced the basics of NumPy and ndarrays. The NumPy library is extensive, including many routines. There are even separate books dedicated to NumPy. For our purposes, we will explore more routines from the NumPy library in the coming chapters as and when we need them for our visualization demonstrations.

The next chapter introduces a few ndarray creation routines and the basics of data visualization with Matplotlib.

CHAPTER 5

Data Visualization with NumPy and Matplotlib

Chapter 4 introduced the basics of NumPy. You learned how to install it and how to create ndarrays. In this chapter, we continue working with NumPy by looking at a few ndarray creation routines. We will also get started with the data visualization library of the scientific computing ecosystem, Matplotlib. We will use the NumPy ndarray creation routines to demonstrate visualizations with Matplotlib. This is a detailed chapter with emphasis on coding and visualizations. The following topics are covered in this chapter:

- Matplotlib

- Visualization with NumPy and Matplotlib

- Single line plots

- Multiline plots

- Grid, axes, and labels

- Colors, styles, and markers

© Ashwin Pajankar 2021
A. Pajankar, *Practical Python Data Visualization*,
https://doi.org/10.1007/978-1-4842-6455-3_5

Throughout the remaining chapters of this book, we will use Matplotlib and NumPy to demonstrate data visualization.

Matplotlib

Matplotlib is an integral part of SciPy and it is used for visualization. It is an extension of NumPy. It provides a MATLAB-like interface for plotting and visualization. It was originally developed by John D Hunter as an open source alternative usable with Python.

We can install it using Jupyter Notebook as follows:

```
!pip3 install matplotlib
```

To use it in the notebook for basic plotting, we must import its `pyplot` module as follows:

```
import matplotlib.pyplot as plt
```

Also, to show the Matplotlib visualizations in the notebook, we must run the following command:

```
%matplotlib inline
```

This forces Matplotlib to show the output inline, directly below the code cell that produces the visualization. We will always use this when we need to use Matplotlib.

Let's import NumPy, too, as follows:

```
import numpy as np
```

You can read more about Matplotlib at `https://matplotlib.org/`.

Visualization with NumPy and Matplotlib

We are now going to learn how to create NumPy ndarrays with ndarray creation routines and then use Matplotlib to visualize them. Let's begin with the routines to create ndarrays.

The first routine is `arange()`. It creates evenly spaced values with the given interval. A stop value argument is compulsory. The start value and interval parameters have default arguments of 0 and 1, respectively. Let's look at an example.

```
x = np.arange(5)
```

In this example, the stop value is 5, so it creates an ndarray starting with 0 and ending at 4. The function returns the sequence that has a half-open interval, which means the stop value is not included in the output. As we have not specified the interval, it assumes it to be 1. We can see the output and the datatype of it as follows:

```
print(x)
type(x)
```

Here is the output:

```
[0 1 2 3 4]
numpy.ndarray
```

Let's go ahead and plot these numbers. For 2D plotting, we need X-Y pairs. Let's keep it simple and say y = f(x) = x by running the following statement:

```
y=x
```

Now, use the function `plot()` to visualize this. It needs the values of X, Y, and the plotting options. We will learn more about the plotting options later in this chapter.

```
plt.plot(x, y, 'o--')
plt.show()
```

The function show() displays the plot. As we can see above, we are visualizing with plotting options o--. This means the points are represented by the solid circles and line is dashed, as shown in Figure 5-1.

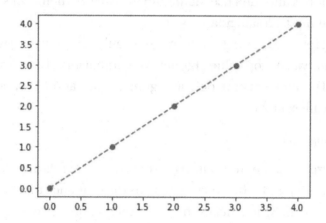

Figure 5-1. *Visualizing y=f(x)=x*

Let's look at an example of the function call for the function arange() with the start and the stop arguments as follows:

```
np.arange(2, 6)
```

It returns the following output (it directly prints and we are not storing it in a variable):

```
array([2, 3, 4, 5])
```

We can even add an argument for the interval as follows:

```
np.arange(2, 6, 2)
```

Here is the output:

```
array([2, 4])
```

The output is displayed in Figure 5-2.

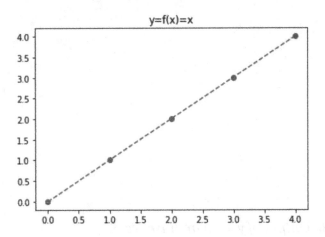

Figure 5-2. *Output with title*

The function linspace(start, stop, number) returns evenly spaced numbers over a specified interval. We must pass it the starting value, the end value, and the number of values as follows:

```
N = 11
x = np.linspace(0, 10, N)
print(x)
```

This code creates 11 numbers (0–10, both inclusive) as follows:

```
[ 0.  1.  2.  3.  4.  5.  6.  7.  8.  9. 10.]
```

We can visualize this as follows:

```
y = x
plt.plot(x, y, 'o--')
plt.axis('off')
plt.show()
```

The output is displayed in Figure 5-3.

Figure 5-3. *Output of y = x with linspace()*

As you can see, we are turning off the axis with the line `plt.axis('off')`.

Similarly, we can compute and visualize values in the `logspace` as follows:

```
y = np.logspace(0.1, 1, N)
print(y)
plt.plot(x, y, 'o--')
plt.show()
```

The output is shown in Figure 5-4.

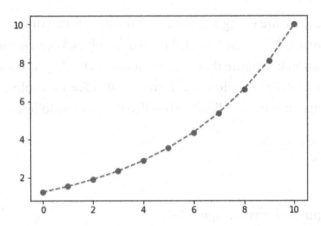

Figure 5-4. *Output of logspace()*

We can even compute a series in the geometric progression as follows:

```
y = np.geomspace(0.1, 1000, N)
print(y)
plt.plot(x, y, 'o--')
plt.show()
```

The output is displayed in Figure 5-5.

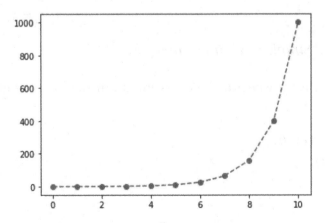

Figure 5-5. *Output of geomspace()*

Single Line Plots

In this section, we are going to explore a few ways we can draw a single line plot. We have used the function plot() to draw plots. When there is only one visualization in a figure that uses the function plot(), then it is known as single line plot. Let's explore this further with a few examples.

We can also use Python lists to visualize the plots as follows:

```
x = [1, 4, 5, 2, 3, 6]
plt.plot(x)
plt.show()
```

The output is shown in Figure 5-6.

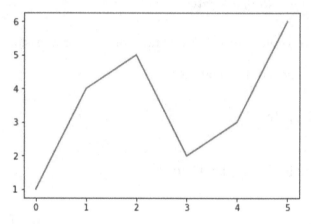

Figure 5-6. *Simple single line graph*

In this case, the values of the y axis are assumed. Here is another example:

```
x = np.arange(10)
plt.plot(x)
plt.show()
```

The output is displayed in Figure 5-7.

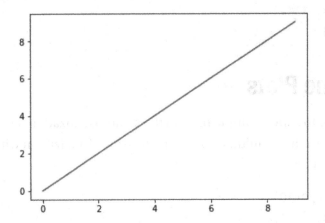

Figure 5-7. *Simple single line graph with arange()*

Next, let's visualize a quadratic graph y = f(x) = x². The code is as follows:

```
plt.plot(x, [y**2 for y in x])
plt.show()
```

The output is shown in Figure 5-8.

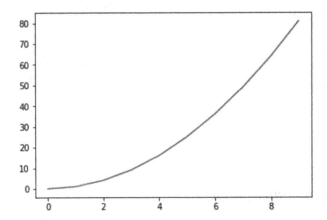

Figure 5-8. $y = f(x) = x^2$

We can write the same code in a simple way:

```
plt.plot(x, x**2)
plt.show()
```

Multiline Plots

It is possible to show multiple plots in the same visualization. Let's look at how we can show multiple curves in the same visualization with this simple example:

```
x = np.arange(10)
plt.plot(x, x**2)
plt.plot(x, x**3)
plt.plot(x, x*2)
plt.plot(x, 2**x)
plt.show()
```

The output is shown in Figure 5-9.

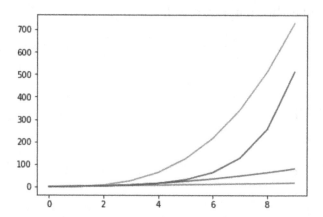

Figure 5-9. *Multiline graph*

As we can see, Matplotlib automatically assigns colors to the curves separately.

We can write the same code in a simple way:

```
plt.plot(x, x**2, x, x**3, x, x*2, x, 2**x)
plt.show()
```

The output will be the same as Figure 5-9.

Here is another example:

```
x = np.array([[1, 2, 6, 3], [4, 5, 3, 2]])
plt.plot(x)
plt.show()
```

The output is displayed in Figure 5-10.

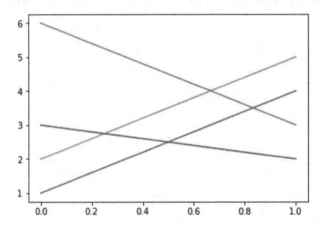

Figure 5-10. *Another example of a multiline graph*

Grid, Axes, and Labels

Earlier, we saw how to enable a grid in the visualizations. It can be done with the statement `plt.grid(True)`. Now we will learn how to manipulate the limits of axes. Before that, though, we will quickly learn how to save a visualization as an image. Look at the following code:

```
x = np.arange(3)
plt.plot(x, x**2, x, x**3, x, 2*x, x, 2**x)
plt.grid(True)
plt.savefig('test.png')
plt.show()
```

The statement `plt.savefig('test.png')` saves the image in the current directory of the Jupyter Notebook file. The output is shown in Figure 5-11.

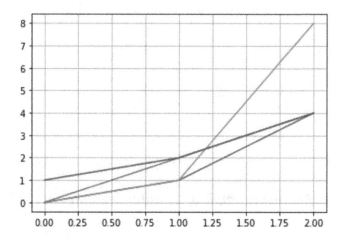

Figure 5-11. *Multiline graph*

We can see that the limits of axes are set by default. We can set them to specific values as shown here:

```
x = np.arange(3)
plt.plot(x, x**2, x, x**3, x, 2*x, x, 2**x)
plt.grid(True)
plt.axis([0, 2, 0, 8])
print(plt.axis())
plt.show()
```

The output is displayed in Figure 5-12.

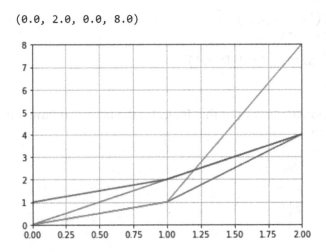

Figure 5-12. *Setting axes*

The statement plt.axis([0, 2, 0, 8]) sets the values of the axes. The first pair (0, 2) refers to the limits for the x axis and the second pair (0, 8) refers to the limits for the y axis. We can write this code with different syntax using the functions xlim() and ylim() as follows:

```
x = np.arange(3)
plt.plot(x, x**2, x, x**3, x, 2*x, x, 2**x)
plt.grid(True)
```

```
plt.xlim([0, 2])
plt.ylim([0, 8])
plt.show()
```

This code produces exactly the same output as Figure 5-12. You can add the title and labels for the axes as follows:

```
x = np.arange(3)
plt.plot(x, x**2, x, x**3, x, 2*x, x, 2**x)
plt.grid(True)
plt.xlabel('x = np.arange(3)')
plt.xlim([0, 2])
plt.ylabel('y = f(x)')
plt.ylim([0, 8])
plt.title('Simple Plot Demo')
plt.show()
```

That produces an output that includes the labels and the title as shown in Figure 5-13.

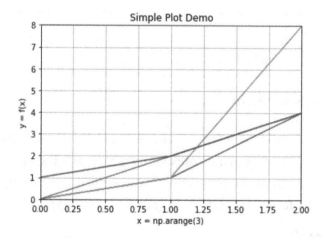

Figure 5-13. *Title and labels for axes*

We can pass an argument for the parameter label in the plot()
function and then call the function legend() to create a legend as follows:

```
x = np.arange(3)
plt.plot(x, x**2, label='x**2')
plt.plot(x, x**3, label='x**3')
plt.plot(x, 2*x, label='2*x')
plt.plot(x, 2**x, label='2**x')
plt.legend()
plt.grid(True)
plt.xlabel('x = np.arange(3)')
plt.xlim([0, 2])
plt.ylabel('y = f(x)')
plt.ylim([0, 8])
plt.title('Simple Plot Demo')
plt.show()
```

That produces an output with legends for the curves as shown in
Figure 5-14.

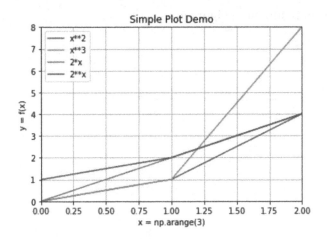

Figure 5-14. *Output with legends*

Instead of passing the legend string as an argument to the function
plot(), we can pass the list of strings as an argument to the function
legend() as follows:

```
x = np.arange(3)
plt.plot(x, x**2, x, x**3, x, 2*x, x, 2**x)
plt.legend(['x**2', 'x**3', '2*x', '2**x'])
plt.grid(True)
plt.xlabel('x = np.arange(3)')
plt.xlim([0, 2])
plt.ylabel('y = f(x)')
plt.ylim([0, 8])
plt.title('Simple Plot Demo')
plt.show()
```

It produces exactly same output as displayed in Figure 5-14.

We can also change the location of the legend box by making the
following change to the preceding code:

```
plt.legend(['x**2', 'x**3', '2*x', '2**x'], loc='upper center')
```

The output is shown in Figure 5-15.

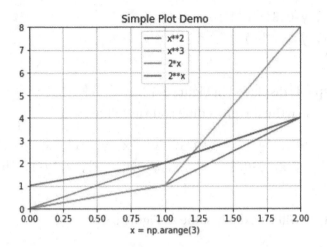

Figure 5-15. *Output with legends in upper middle position*

Colors, Styles, and Markers

Thus far, in case of multiline plots, we have seen that Matplotlib automatically assigns colors, styles, and markers. We have also seen a few examples of customizing them. In this section, we will look at how to customize them in detail.

Let's start with colors. The following code lists all the primary colors supported by Matplotlib (we are not customizing styles and markers in this example).

```
x = np.arange(5)
y = x
plt.plot(x, y+1, 'g')
plt.plot(x, y+0.5, 'y')
plt.plot(x, y, 'r')
plt.plot(x, y-0.2, 'c')
plt.plot(x, y-0.4, 'k')
plt.plot(x, y-0.6, 'm')
```

```
plt.plot(x, y-0.8, 'w')
plt.plot(x, y-1, 'b')
plt.show()
```

The output is displayed in Figure 5-16.

We can also write the preceding code as follows:

```
plt.plot(x, y+1, 'g', x, y+0.5, 'y', x, y, 'r', x, y-0.2, 'c',
x, y-0.4, 'k', x, y-0.6, 'm', x, y-0.8, 'w', x, y-1, 'b')
plt.show()
```

The output will be exactly same as Figure 5-16.

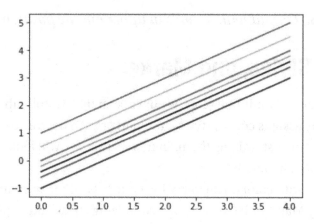

Figure 5-16. *Demo of colors*

We can customize the line style as follows:

```
plt.plot(x, y, '-', x, y+1, '--', x, y+2, '-.', x, y+3, ':')
plt.show()
```

The output is shown in Figure 5-17.

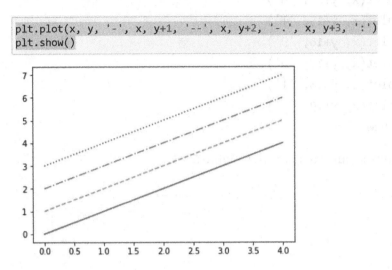

Figure 5-17. *Line styles*

You can even change the markers as follows:

```
plt.plot(x, y, '.')
plt.plot(x, y+0.5, ',')
plt.plot(x, y+1, 'o')
plt.plot(x, y+2, '<')
plt.plot(x, y+3, '>')
plt.plot(x, y+4, 'v')
plt.plot(x, y+5, '^')
plt.plot(x, y+6, '1')
plt.plot(x, y+7, '2')
plt.plot(x, y+8, '3')
plt.plot(x, y+9, '4')
plt.plot(x, y+10, 's')
plt.plot(x, y+11, 'p')
plt.plot(x, y+12, '*')
```

```
plt.plot(x, y+13, 'h')
plt.plot(x, y+14, 'H')
plt.plot(x, y+15, '+')
plt.plot(x, y+16, 'D')
plt.plot(x, y+17, 'd')
plt.plot(x, y+18, '|')
plt.plot(x, y+19, '_')
plt.show()
```

The output is displayed in Figure 5-18.

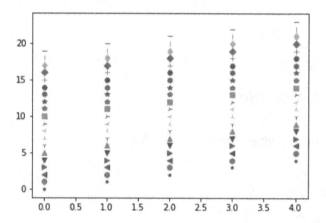

Figure 5-18. *Markers*

All three features (colors, markers, and line styles) can be combined to customize the visualization as follows:

```
plt.plot(x, y, 'mo--')
plt.plot(x, y+1 , 'g*-.')
plt.show()
```

The output is shown in Figure 5-19.

```
plt.plot(x, y, 'mo--')
plt.plot(x, y+1 , 'g*-.')
plt.show()
```

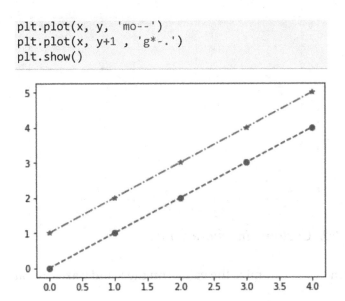

Figure 5-19. *Customizing everything*

These are basic customizations, but you can customize everything in greater detail. For example, use this code to customize other details:

```
plt.plot(x, y, color='g', linestyle='--', linewidth=1.5,
        marker='^', markerfacecolor='b', markeredgecolor='k',
        markeredgewidth=1.5, markersize=5)
plt.grid(True)
plt.show()
```

The output is shown in Figure 5-20.

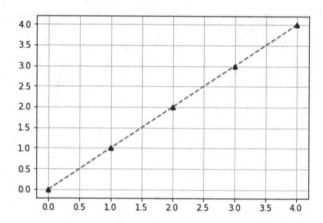

Figure 5-20. *Customizing more details*

You can even customize the values on the x and y axes as follows:

```
x = y = np.arange(10)
plt.plot(x, y, 'o--')
plt.xticks(range(len(x)), ['a', 'b', 'c', 'd', 'e', 'f', 'g',
'h', 'i', 'j'])
plt.yticks(range(0, 10, 1))
plt.show()
```

The output is displayed in Figure 5-21.

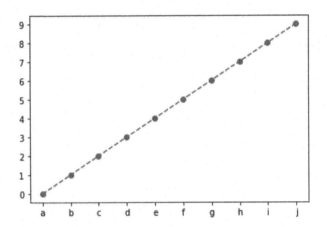

Figure 5-21.   *Customizing the ticks on axes*

Summary

This chapter focused on the various customizations available for visualizations. We learned a great deal about visualizing data. The concepts covered in this chapter will be used throughout this book to visualize data.

In the next chapter, we will explore data visualization even further. We will learn to visualize images and 3D shapes and look at the basics of operations of images.

CHAPTER 6

Visualizing Images and 3D Shapes

In Chapter 5, we got started with visualization using the Matplotlib library in Python 3. In this chapter, we will continue our adventures with Matplotlib and NumPy to visualize images and 3D shapes. Let's continue our exploration of data visualization with the following topics:

- Visualizing the images

- Operations on images

- 3D visualizations

After this chapter, you will be able to work with images and 3D Shapes.

Visualizing the Images

In this section, we will learn how to visualize images. We will start by creating a new notebook for this chapter. Matplotlib's function `imread()` can read images in `.png` file format. To enable it to read files other formats, you must install another image processing library known as pillow. Install it by running the following command in the notebook cell:

```
!pip3 install pillow
```

© Ashwin Pajankar 2021
A. Pajankar, *Practical Python Data Visualization*,
https://doi.org/10.1007/978-1-4842-6455-3_6

Use the magic command we discussed in Chapter 5 to enable the notebook to show Matplotlib visualizations:

```
%matplotlib inline
```

Import Matplotlib's Pyplot module with the following command:

```
import matplotlib.pyplot as plt
```

Now, let's read an image into a variable using the function imread() as follows:

```
img1 = plt.imread('D:\\Dataset\\4.1.02.tiff')
```

If you are using a Linux, Unix, or MacOS computer, then you need to use the following convention for the file path.

```
img1 = plt.imread('/home/pi/book/dataset/4.1.02.tiff')
```

The path you are using must be an absolute path. If the image file is in the same directory as the program, then the name of only the file will suffice.

This function reads an image and stores it in a NumPy ndarray as matrix of numerical values. We can verify this by running the following line of code:

```
print(type(img1))
```

The output is as follows:

```
<class 'numpy.ndarray'>
```

This confirms that the scientific Python libraries handle images as NumPy ndarrays.

We can show the image with Matplotlib's imshow() function and then display it as a figure with the function show() as follows:

```
plt.imshow(img1)
plt.show()
```

The output is shown in Figure 6-1.

Figure 6-1. *Visualizing a color image*

You can turn the axis off as follows:

```
plt.imshow(img1)
plt.axis(False)
plt.show()
```

Note   All the images I am using for the demonstration are downloaded from http://www.imageprocessingplace.com/ root_files_V3/image_databases.htm.

Let's read a grayscale image as follows:

```
img2 = plt.imread('D:\\Dataset\\5.3.01.tiff')
```

We can show it using this code:

```
plt.imshow(img2)
plt.axis(False)
plt.show()
```

Figure 6-2 displays the output.

Figure 6-2. *Visualizing a grayscale image with the default color map*

As you can see, the colors seem a bit strange, and this is not a color image at all. Matplotlib is displaying the grayscale image with the default color map. We can assign the gray color map explicitly to visualize this image properly as follows:

```
plt.imshow(img2, cmap=plt.cm.gray)
plt.axis(False)
plt.show()
```

Figure 6-3 displays the result.

Figure 6-3. *Visualizing a grayscale image with the gray color map*

We can also indicate the color map as follows:

```
plt.imshow(img2, cmap='gray')
plt.axis(False)
plt.show()
```

Next we turn to basic operations with images.

Operations on Images

We can perform basic operations on images with NumPy and visualize the outputs with Matplotlib. First let's learn a few arithmetic operations. We need two images with the same dimensions for arithmetic operations. Let us read another color image as follows:

```
img3 = plt.imread('D:\\Dataset\\4.1.03.tiff')
```

We can visualize it as follows:

```
plt.imshow(img3)
plt.axis(False)
plt.show()
```

Figure 6-4 shows the output.

Figure 6-4. *Another color image for image operations*

We can add two images and visualize them as follows:

```
add = img1+img3
plt.imshow(add)
plt.axis(False)
plt.show()
```

Figure 6-5 displays the output.

Figure 6-5. *Addition of two images*

The addition operation is a commutative arithmetic operation. This means that if we change the order of the operands, it will not affect the output.

```
add1 = img3+img1
plt.imshow(add)
plt.axis(False)
plt.show()
```

Let's try a subtraction operation:

```
sub1= img1-img3
plt.imshow(sub1)
plt.axis(False)
plt.show()
```

Figure 6-6 shows the output.

Figure 6-6.   *Result of subtraction*

We know that the subtraction operation is not commutative. This means that if we change the order of operands, then the result is different. Let's try that:

```
sub1 = img3-img1
plt.imshow(sub1)
plt.axis(False)
plt.show()
```

The output shown in Figure 6-7 is therefore different than the previous output (Figure 6-6).

Figure 6-7. *Result of subtraction*

We have learned that the images are represented as NumPy ndarrays in SciPy. The difference between color and grayscale images is that color images are made up of multiple channels. These channels are ndarrays themselves. We can split the color images and visualize the constituent channels separately using indexing in NumPy. Color images have one channel for each of the colors red, green, and blue. You can split an image with NumPy indexing as follows:

```
r = img3[:, :, 0]
g = img3[:, :, 1]
b = img3[:, :, 2]
```

Let's visualize the original image and the color channels using the subplots in Matplotlib:

```
plt.subplots_adjust(hspace=0.4, wspace=0.1)
plt.subplot(2, 2, 1)
plt.title('Original')
```

```
plt.imshow(img3)

plt.subplot(2, 2, 2)
plt.title('Red')
plt.imshow(r, cmap='gray')

plt.subplot(2, 2, 3)
plt.title('Green')
plt.imshow(g, cmap='gray')

plt.subplot(2, 2, 4)
plt.title('Blue')
plt.imshow(b, cmap='gray')

plt.show()
```

Let's examine the preceding code. You are creating a grid of 2 × 2 using the function subplot(). The function subplots_adjust() is used to adjust distance between the visualizations. The top left position in the 2 × 2 grid is 1, the adjacent position in the same row is 2, and so on. The bottom right position is the fourth position. Using the function subplot() before imshow() or plot(), we can decide where the visualization must be placed. The output is shown in Figure 6-8.

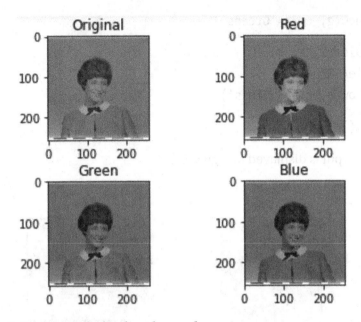

Figure 6-8. *Separated color channels*

The color channels themselves are 2D matrices with the values of the members ranging from 0 to 256 for an 8-bit unsigned integer representation format of a color image. When they are combined, Matplotlib interprets them as a color image. We can use appropriate color maps to visualize this as follows:

```
plt.subplots_adjust(hspace=0.4, wspace=0.1)
plt.subplot(2, 2, 1)
plt.title('Original')
plt.imshow(img3)

plt.subplot(2, 2, 2)
plt.title('Red')
plt.imshow(r, cmap='Reds')

plt.subplot(2, 2, 3)
plt.title('Green')
```

```
plt.imshow(g, cmap='Greens')

plt.subplot(2, 2, 4)
plt.title('Blue')
plt.imshow(b, cmap='Blues')

plt.show()
```

The output is displayed in Figure 6-9.

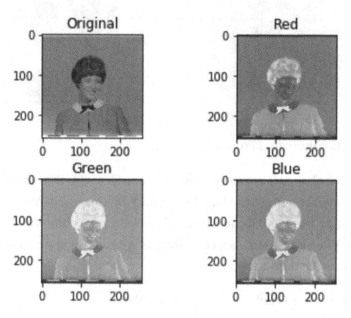

Figure 6-9. *Separated color channels visualized with appropriate color maps*

We can combine the constituent channels to form the original image using the following code:

```
import numpy as np
img4 = np.dstack((r, g, b))
```

We are using the function dstack() from the NumPy library. We can visualize the output with the usual code:

```
plt.imshow(img4)
plt.axis(False)
plt.show()
```

This is how you can perform very basic image processing operations. There is more to image processing than what we have learned, and further demonstrations would warrant a separate book.

3D Visualizations

In this section, we examine 3D visualizations with Python 3. To this point, we have been displaying the visualizations in the notebook itself. This process works well for 2D visualizations. In the case of 3D visualizations, though, it will show them only with a fixed angle. We therefore must use another method. The best way to work with this is to use another magic command that shows a visualization in a separate Qt window as follows:

```
%matplotlib qt
```

We have already imported the pyplot module in Matplotlib and NumPy in the earlier cells (I am assuming you will continue using the same notebook for the whole chapter). We must import more functionality with the following statements:

```
from mpl_toolkits.mplot3d import Axes3D
from mpl_toolkits.mplot3d import axes3d
```

Let's start with something simple. We have seen how to draw simple plots, so now we will do the same in 3D. Begin with a simple parametric curve. First define the figure and axis:

```
fig = plt.figure()
ax = fig.gca(projection='3d')
```

For 3D visualizations we have enabled 3D projections with the parameter and argument pair projection='3d'. Next, define the data. You need the x, y, and z coordinates of the data points. First define polar coordinates of the data points as follows:

```
theta = np.linspace(-3 * np.pi, 3 * np.pi, 200)
z = np.linspace(-3, 3, 200)
r = z**3 + 1
```

Now, compute x and y coordinates as follows:

```
x = r * np.sin(theta)
y = r * np.cos(theta)
```

We are using the trigonometric functions in the NumPy library to compute x and y. Finally, let's plot it as follows:

```
ax.plot(x, y, z, label='Parametric Curve')
ax.legend()
plt.show()
```

The output will be displayed in a separate window as shown in Figure 6-10, and it will be interactive in such a way that we will be able to change the angle of view.

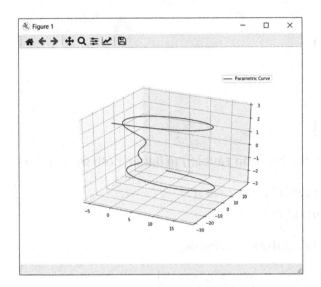

Figure 6-10. *Visualizing a parametric curve*

Note   If a separate output window does not pop up and the 3D visualization is shown in the browser itself, then you must restart the Jupyter kernel and reexecute the relevant cells. In that case, do not execute the cell containing %matplotlib inline.

Next, let's create a 3D bar graph. Compute the data now as follows:

```
x = np.arange(4)
y = np.arange(4)
xx, yy = np.meshgrid(x, y)
print(xx);print(yy)
```

The function meshgrid() creates and returns coordinate matrices from coordinate vectors as follows:

```
[[0 1 2 3]
 [0 1 2 3]
```

```
 [0 1 2 3]
 [0 1 2 3]]
[[0 0 0 0]
 [1 1 1 1]
 [2 2 2 2]
 [3 3 3 3]]
```

Then use the function ravel() to flatten both the matrices as follows:

```
X, Y = xx.ravel(), yy.ravel()
print(X); print(Y);
```

This results in the following output:

```
[0 1 2 3 0 1 2 3 0 1 2 3 0 1 2 3]
[0 0 0 0 1 1 1 1 2 2 2 2 3 3 3 3]
```

Now, compute more values:

```
top = X + Y
bottom = np.zeros_like(top)
width = depth = 1
```

Next, create a figure and axes and create the bar graph as follows:

```
fig = plt.figure(figsize=(8, 3))
ax1 = fig.add_subplot(121, projection='3d')
ax2 = fig.add_subplot(122, projection='3d')
ax1.bar3d(X, Y, bottom, width, depth, top, shade=True)
ax1.set_title('Shaded')
ax2.bar3d(X, Y, bottom, width, depth, top, shade=False)
ax2.set_title('Not Shaded')
plt.show()
```

This produces the bar graph shown in Figure 6-11.

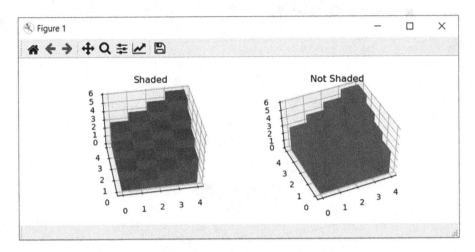

Figure 6-11. *Visualizing a 3D bar graph*

Next let's visualize a wireframe as follows:

```
fig = plt.figure()
ax = fig.gca(projection='3d')
X, Y, Z = axes3d.get_test_data(delta=0.1)
ax.plot_wireframe(X, Y, Z)
plt.show()
```

In this code snippet, we first create a figure and an axis in 3D mode. Then the built-in function get_test_data() returns the test data. Next we use the function plot_wireframe() to plot the wireframe model. The output is shown in Figure 6-12.

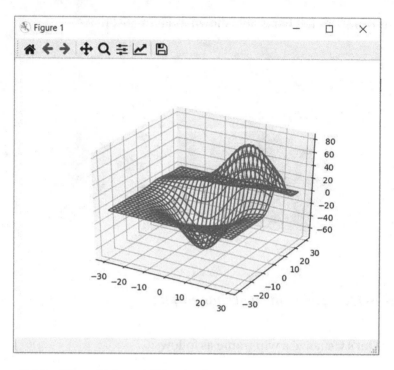

Figure 6-12. *Visualizing a 3D wireframe*

Finally, let's compute and visualize a surface. First, compute the x and y coordinates and then compute the mesh grid:

```
x = np.arange(-3, 3, 0.09)
y = np.arange(-3, 3, 0.09)
X, Y = np.meshgrid(x, y)
print(X); print(Y)
```

The output is as follows:

```
[[-3.   -2.91 -2.82 ...  2.76  2.85  2.94]
 [-3.   -2.91 -2.82 ...  2.76  2.85  2.94]
 [-3.   -2.91 -2.82 ...  2.76  2.85  2.94]
 ...
 [-3.   -2.91 -2.82 ...  2.76  2.85  2.94]
```

```
 [-3.    -2.91 -2.82 ...  2.76  2.85  2.94]
 [-3.    -2.91 -2.82 ...  2.76  2.85  2.94]]
[[-3.    -3.    -3.    ... -3.    -3.    -3.  ]
 [-2.91 -2.91 -2.91 ... -2.91 -2.91 -2.91]
 [-2.82 -2.82 -2.82 ... -2.82 -2.82 -2.82]
 ...
 [ 2.76  2.76  2.76 ...  2.76  2.76  2.76]
 [ 2.85  2.85  2.85 ...  2.85  2.85  2.85]
 [ 2.94  2.94  2.94 ...  2.94  2.94  2.94]]
```

Next, compute the z coordinate as follows:

```
R = np.sqrt(X**2 + Y**2)
Z = np.cos(R)
print(Z)
```

Finally, create the figure and axis, and visualize the 3D surface:

```
fig = plt.figure()
ax = fig.gca(projection='3d')
surf = ax.plot_surface(X, Y, Z,
                        cmap=plt.cm.cool,
                        linewidth=0,
                        antialiased=False)
plt.show()
```

This produces the output shown in Figure 6-13.

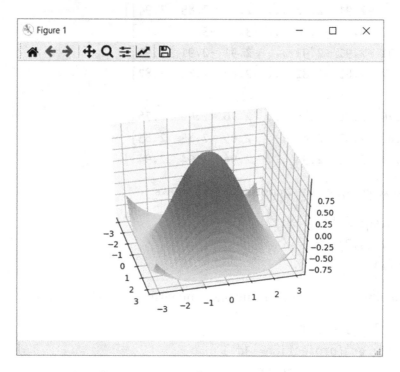

Figure 6-13. *Visualizing a 3D surface*

Summary

In this chapter, you learned about and demonstrated visualizing images. You also learned about and demonstrated basic operations on images such as arithmetic operations and splitting the color images into constituent channels. We also covered writing programs for 3D visualizations including curves, bars, wireframes, and meshes.

The next chapter explores how to visualize networks and graph data structures.

CHAPTER 7

Visualizing Graphs and Networks

In Chapter 6, we demonstrated the visualization of images and 3D objects with Python 3 and Matplotlib. We also learned a bit of image processing.

This chapter focuses on the visualization of the data structure known as a graph or a network. Let's continue our data visualization journey with the following topics:

- Graphs and networks

- Visualizing graphs in Python 3

- More types of graphs

- Assigning custom labels to nodes

After completing this chapter, you will be able to visualize graphs and networks with Python 3.

Graphs and Networks

A graph is an abstract datatype. It is also known as a network. It consists of a finite set of vertices (also known as nodes) and a finite set of edges (also known as links). The terms vertices and edges are used when we refer to a graph. Nodes and links are the terms used when we refer to the same

© Ashwin Pajankar 2021

A. Pajankar, *Practical Python Data Visualization*,
https://doi.org/10.1007/978-1-4842-6455-3_7

structure as a network. Throughout the chapter, I use the terms graphs, nodes, and edges to refer this data structure for consistency.

In a graph, vertices are connected to each other by edges. Trees are subtype of graphs. In graphs we can have cycles, but in trees we cannot. We can also have directed graphs and undirected graphs. Edges can be assigned with values in the graphs, and such graphs are known as weighted graphs. In this chapter, we discuss visualization of undirected and unweighted graphs.

Graphs in Python 3

To work and visualize with graphs, there is an easy-to-use library for Python 3, known as networkx. You can install it by running the following command in a Jupyter Notebook cell:

```
!pip3 install network
```

Now, import it and the other library, Matplotlib. We also will enable plotting in the notebook:

```
%matplotlib inline
import networkx as nx
import matplotlib.pyplot as plt
```

You can create a new empty graph as follows:

```
G = nx.Graph()
```

Let us determine its type as follows:

```
type(G)
```

Here is the output:

```
networkx.classes.graph.Graph
```

You can see the list of nodes and edges, and you can also see their datatype as follows:

```
print(G.nodes())
print(G.edges())
print(type(G.nodes()))
print(type(G.edges()))
```

This produces the following output:

```
[]
[]
<class 'networkx.classes.reportviews.NodeView'>
<class 'networkx.classes.reportviews.EdgeView'>
```

You can add a node as follows:

```
G.add_node('a')
```

Alternatively, you can also add multiple nodes specified in a list:

```
G.add_nodes_from(['b', 'c'])
```

We will again print the list of nodes and the list of edges (which should be empty, as we have not added any edges yet):

```
print('Nodes of the graph G: ')
print(G.nodes())
print('Edges of the graph G: ')
print(G.edges())
```

The output looks like this:

```
Nodes of the graph G:
['a', 'b', 'c']
Edges of the graph G:
[]
```

Look at the following statement:

```
G.add_edge(1, 2)
```

It adds two nodes and a corresponding edge. If the argument in the function call is already part of the list of nodes of the graph, then it is not added twice. The following is another way to add it:

```
edge = ('d', 'e')
G.add_edge(*edge)
edge = ('a', 'b')
G.add_edge(*edge)
```

Let's again print the list of nodes and edges as follows:

```
print('Nodes of the graph G: ')
print(G.nodes())
print('Edges of the graph G: ')
print(G.edges())
```

We can also specify the list of edges and add it to the graph:

```
G.add_edges_from([('a', 'c'), ('c', 'd'),
                  ('a', 1), (1, 'd'),
                  ('a', 2)])
```

Now let's print everything again:

```
print('Nodes of the graph G: ')
print(G.nodes())
print('Edges of the graph G: ')
print(G.edges())
```

The output is as follows:

```
Nodes of the graph G:
['a', 'b', 'c', 1, 2, 'd', 'e']
Edges of the graph G:
[('a', 'b'), ('a', 'c'), ('a', 1), ('a', 2), ('c', 'd'), (1,
2), (1, 'd'), ('d', 'e')]
```

Visualizing Graphs in Python 3

This section focuses on visualization of the graphs with networkx library. You already prepared a graph in the earlier section. Now you can just visualize it as follows:

```
nx.draw(G)
plt.show()
```

The output is shown in Figure 7-1.

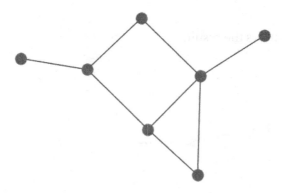

Figure 7-1. *Visual representation of the graph*

Note that these visualizations are generated randomly and every time we run the statement, it creates a different image for the visual representation. However, the graphs represented by these visualizations are isomorphic. Figure 7-2 shows the output when you execute the same cell again.

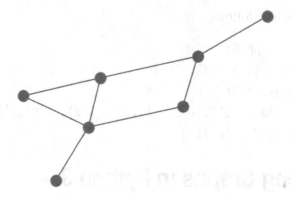

Figure 7-2. *Another visual representation of the same graph*

You can see that the both visualizations are isomorphic, as they are generated from the same graph. You must also have observed that the nodes do not display any names. You can show the names of the nodes with the following code:

```
nx.draw(G, with_labels=True)
plt.show()
```

Figure 7-3 shows the result.

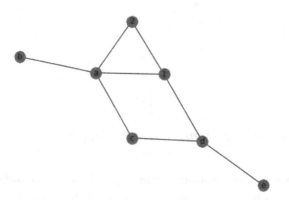

Figure 7-3. *Nodes with labels*

To display the labels of the nodes in bold type, use this code:

```
nx.draw(G, with_labels=True, font_weight='bold')
plt.show()
```

The visualization looks Figure 7-4.

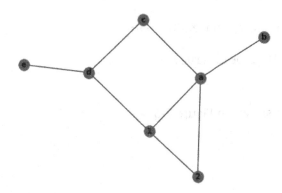

Figure 7-4. *Nodes with bold labels*

More Types of Graphs

Next, we can look at a few more types of graphs and their visualizations. The first one is a linear graph or path graph. The number of nodes connected to a node in a graph is known as the degree of that node. We can say that a path graph is a graph that has two nodes of degree one and the rest of the nodes have degree two. If we arrange a path graph visually, it looks like a segmented line. To create a path graph, run the following code:

```
G = nx.path_graph(4)
```

To display the nodes and edges, use this code:

```
print('Nodes of the graph G: ')
print(G.nodes())
print('Edges of the graph G: ')
print(G.edges())
```

Here is the output:

```
Nodes of the graph G:
[0, 1, 2, 3]
Edges of the graph G:
[(0, 1), (1, 2), (2, 3)]
```

Next, let's create a visualization of it:

```
nx.draw(G, with_labels=True)
plt.show()
```

The result is shown in Figure 7-5.

Figure 7-5. *Path graph with four nodes*

The next type of graph is the Petersen graph, an undirected graph with 10 vertices and 15 edges. We can create it and see the values of edges and nodes using the following code:

```
G = nx.petersen_graph()
print('Nodes of the graph G: ')
print(G.nodes())
print('Edges of the graph G: ')
print(G.edges())
```

We can visualize it as follows:

```
nx.draw(G, with_labels=True)
plt.show()
```

The output is shown in Figure 7-6.

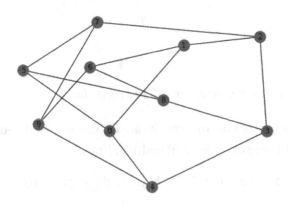

Figure 7-6. *Petersen graph*

Now, there are many ways to depict it better. We could depict it as a pentagon with a pentagram inside, with five spokes. The following code does that.

```
nx.draw_shell(G, nlist=[range(5, 10),
                        range(5)],
             with_labels=True,
             font_weight='bold')
plt.show()
```

This code shows it in a shell form. We are mentioning the layer-wise lists of nodes in the argument nlist. The output displayed in Figure 7-7 is isomorphic to the preceding output.

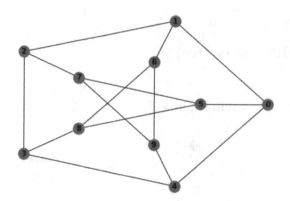

Figure 7-7. *Petersen graph visualized as a shell*

We can customize how our graphs are depicted. Use the following code to customize the size of nodes and width of lines:

```
options = {'node_color': 'black', 'node_size': 100, 'width': 3}
```

Now let's visualize the Petersen graph with these options:

```
nx.draw_random(G, **options)
plt.show()
```

Figure 7-8 displays the output.

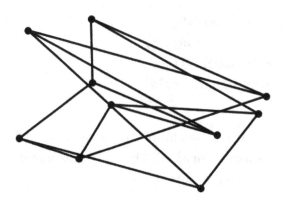

Figure 7-8. *Petersen graph with customized nodes and edges*

Next, we can visualize it in a circular configuration as follows:

```
nx.draw_circular(G, **options)
plt.show()
```

The output is shown in Figure 7-9.

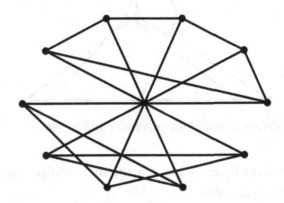

Figure 7-9. *Petersen graph in circular configuration*

We can also depict the Petersen graph in a spectral configuration as follows:

```
nx.draw_spectral(G, **options)
plt.show()
```

Figure 7-10 displays the output.

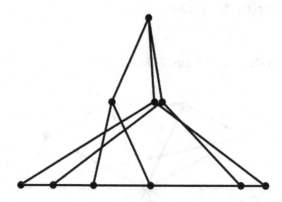

Figure 7-10. *Petersen graph in spectral configuration*

We can depict the Petersen graph in the shell configuration with customized options as follows:

```
nx.draw_shell(G, nlist=[range(5, 10), range(5)], **options)
plt.show()
```

The output is displayed in Figure 7-11.

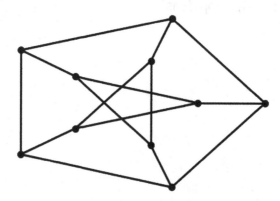

Figure 7-11. *Petersen graph in shell configuration with custom nodes and edges*

We can also create a dodecahedral graph as follows:

```
G = nx.dodecahedral_graph()
```

It can be visualized in the shell form as follows:

```
shells = [[2, 3, 4, 5, 6],
          [8, 1, 0, 19, 18,
           17, 16, 15, 14, 7],
          [9, 10, 11, 12, 13]]
nx.draw_shell(G, nlist=shells, **options)
plt.show()
```

Figure 7-12 displays the output.

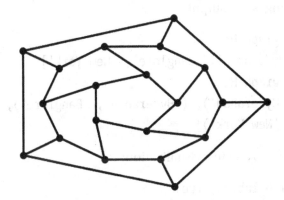

Figure 7-12. *Dodecahedral graph in shell configuration with custom nodes and edges*

You can save any graph figures as a files on the disk using this command:

```
plt.savefig('graph.png')
```

This statement saves a file on the disk in the location of the program (the same directory as the notebook).

Assigning Custom Labels to Nodes

You can use the following code to assign custom labels to the nodes:

```
G = nx.path_graph(4)
cities = {0: 'Mumbai', 1: 'Hyderabad',
          2: 'Banglore', 3: 'New York'}
H=nx.relabel_nodes(G, cities)

print('Nodes of the graph H: ')
print(H.nodes())
print('Edges of the graph H: ')
print(H.edges())
```

The following is the output:

```
Nodes of the graph H:
['Mumbai', 'Hyderabad', 'Banglore', 'New York']
Edges of the graph H:
[('Mumbai', 'Hyderabad'), ('Hyderabad', 'Banglore'),
('Banglore', 'New York')]
```

Use this code to create a visualization:

```
nx.draw(H, with_labels=True)
plt.show()
```

Figure 7-13 displays the output.

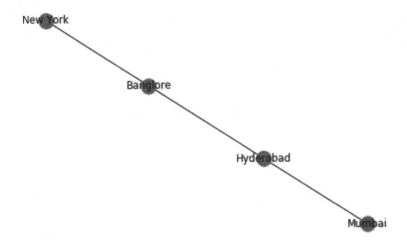

Figure 7-13. *Relabeled nodes in a linear or path graph*

Summary

This chapter explored the concept of graphs, introducing different types. You learned to visualize them in different ways. Now you should be comfortable with visualization of the graph data structures in Python 3.

The next chapter covers the data science library of SciPy, pandas. We introduce versatile data structures in the pandas library, series and dataframe, along with a few examples of data visualization.

CHAPTER 8

Getting Started with Pandas

Chapter 7 covered the visualization of graphs using the Python library networkx. This chapter focuses on the basics of the data science and analytics library of SciPy, pandas. First, we will explore the data structures in this library. You will also learn how to read the data from a .csv data set. Finally, you will learn how to create simple demonstrations of visualizations. These are the topics that are covered in the chapter:

- Introduction to pandas

- Dataframe in pandas

- Visualizing with pandas

After you complete this chapter, you should be comfortable with basic visualizations using pandas.

Introduction to Pandas

Pandas is the data analytics component and an integral part of the SciPy ecosystem. It includes very versatile data structures and routines to manage them. It also has the capability to visualize the data in a scientific data format.

© Ashwin Pajankar 2021
A. Pajankar, *Practical Python Data Visualization*,
https://doi.org/10.1007/978-1-4842-6455-3_8

The first step is to install it on the computer by running the following command in Jupyter Notebook:

```
!pip3 install pandas
```

You can import it to the current session by running the following command:

```
import pandas as pd
```

You can read more about pandas at https://pandas.pydata.org/.

Series in Pandas

A series is a one-dimensional array with labels. It can hold data of any type. The labels are collectively known as the index.

We can create a series as follows:

```
s1 = pd.Series([1, 2, 3 , 5, -3])
```

To determine its datatypes, use the following command:

```
type(s1)
```

You can see the values and index associated with them using the following statement:

```
print(s1)
```

You can explicitly mention the datatype as follows:

```
s2 = pd.Series([1, 2, 3 , 5, -3], dtype=np.int32)
print(s2)
```

To pass a list as an argument to the constructor function to create a series, use this code:

```
x = [1, 2, 3 , 5, -3]
s3 = pd.Series(x)
```

We can even pass a NumPy ndarray as an argument to the constructor function to create a series as follows:

```
Import numpy as np
y = np.array(x)
s4 = pd.Series(y)
```

To display the values, use this code:

```
print(s4.values)
```

This provides the following output:

```
[ 1  2  3  5 -3]
```

You can retrieve the index as follows:

```
print(s4.index)
```

This results in the following output:

```
RangeIndex(start=0, stop=5, step=1)
```

To assign a custom index, use the following code:

```
s5 = pd.Series( x, index = ['a', 'b', 'c', 'd', 'e'])
print(s5)
```

This provides the following output:

```
a    1
b    2
c    3
```

```
d    5
e    -3
dtype: int64
```

Basic Operations on Series

We can perform a few basic operations on series. For example, we can display the negative numbers as follows:

```
print(s5[s5 < 0])
```

This results in the following output:

```
e    -3
dtype: int64
```

We can also retrieve the positive numbers as follows:

```
print(s5[s5 > 0])
```

The output is shown here:

```
a    1
b    2
c    3
d    5
dtype: int64
```

These are examples of comparison operations. To perform a multiplication operation, use this syntax:

```
c = 3
print ( s5 * c )
```

The output is as follows:

```
a    3
b    6
c    9
d    15
e    -9
dtype: int64
```

Dataframes in Pandas

A dataframe is a two-dimensional labeled data structure with columns of that can be of different datatypes. We can create dataframes from series, ndarrays, lists, and dictionaries.

Dataframes have labels and they are collectively referred to as an index. We can easily view and manipulate data in the dataframes. The data is stored in a rectangular grid format in dataframes.

We can create a dataframe from a list of dictionary data as follows:

```
data = {'city': ['Mumbai', 'Mumbai', 'Mumbai',
                 'Hyderabad', 'Hyderabad', 'Hyderabad'],
        'year': [2010, 2011, 2012, 2010, 2011, 2012,],
        'population': [10.0, 10.1, 10.2, 5.2, 5.3, 5.5]}
```

To create a dataframe from this, use the following code:

```
df1 = pd.DataFrame(data)
print(df1)
```

The output is as follows:

```
        city  year  population
0      Mumbai  2010        10.0
1      Mumbai  2011        10.1
2      Mumbai  2012        10.2
3   Hyderabad  2010         5.2
4   Hyderabad  2011         5.3
5   Hyderabad  2012         5.5
```

Use the following line of code to display the top five records:

```
df1.head()
```

The output is as follows:

```
        city  year  population
0      Mumbai  2010        10.0
1      Mumbai  2011        10.1
2      Mumbai  2012        10.2
3   Hyderabad  2010         5.2
4   Hyderabad  2011         5.3
```

You can also pass other numbers as arguments to the function head() and it will show that number of the top records from the dataframe. Similarly, you can use df1.tail() to show the last records. It has 5 as the default argument, but you can customize the argument passed to it.

You can create a dataframe with a particular order of columns as follows:

```
df2 = pd.DataFrame(data, columns=['year', 'city',
'population'])
print(df2)
```

This results in the following output:

```
   year       city  population
0  2010     Mumbai        10.0
1  2011     Mumbai        10.1
2  2012     Mumbai        10.2
3  2010  Hyderabad         5.2
4  2011  Hyderabad         5.3
5  2012  Hyderabad         5.5
```

Next let's create a dataframe with an additional column and custom index:

```
df3 = pd.DataFrame(data, columns=['year', 'city', 'population',
'GDP'],
                    index = ['one', 'two', 'three', 'four',
                    'five', 'six'])
print(df3)
```

The following is the new dataframe:

```
       year       city  population  GDP
one    2010     Mumbai        10.0  NaN
two    2011     Mumbai        10.1  NaN
three  2012     Mumbai        10.2  NaN
four   2010  Hyderabad         5.2  NaN
five   2011  Hyderabad         5.3  NaN
six    2012  Hyderabad         5.5  NaN
```

Use the following command to print the list of columns:

```
print(df3.columns)
```

Here is the resulting output:

```
Index(['year', 'city', 'population', 'GDP'], dtype='object')
```

We can print the list of indexes as follows:

```
print(df3.index)
```

That provides the following output:

```
Index(['one', 'two', 'three', 'four', 'five', 'six'],
dtype='object')
```

You can display the data of a column with the following statement:

```
print(df3.year)
```

Alternatively, you can also use the following statement:

```
print(df3['year'])
```

Here is the output:

```
one        2010
two        2011
three      2012
four       2010
five       2011
six        2012
Name: year, dtype: int64
```

You can display the datatype of a column with the following statement:

```
print(df3['year'].dtype)
```

You can also use this code:

```
print(df3.year.dtype)
```

That provides the following output:

```
int64
```

To display the datatype of all the columns, use this statement:

```
print(df3.dtypes)
```

The output is as follows:

```
year              int64
city             object
population      float64
GDP              object
dtype: object
```

We can retrieve any record using the index as follows:

```
df3.loc['one']
```

Here is the resulting output:

```
year              2010
city            Mumbai
population          10
GDP                NaN
Name: one, dtype: object
```

You can assign the same value to all the members of a column as follows:

```
df3.GDP = 10
print(df3)
```

The output is shown here:

```
        year        city  population  GDP
one     2010      Mumbai        10.0   10
two     2011      Mumbai        10.1   10
three   2012      Mumbai        10.2   10
four    2010   Hyderabad         5.2   10
```

```
five    2011  Hyderabad           5.3    10
six     2012  Hyderabad           5.5    10
```

We can assign an ndarray to the GDP column as follows:

```
import numpy as np
df3.GDP = np.arange(6)
print(df3)
```

That gives the following output:

	year	city	population	GDP
one	2010	Mumbai	10.0	0
two	2011	Mumbai	10.1	1
three	2012	Mumbai	10.2	2
four	2010	Hyderabad	5.2	3
five	2011	Hyderabad	5.3	4
six	2012	Hyderabad	5.5	5

You can also assign it a list as follows:

```
df3.GDP = [3, 2, 0, 9, -0.4, 7]
print(df3)
```

The output is as follows:

	year	city	population	GDP
one	2010	Mumbai	10.0	3.0
two	2011	Mumbai	10.1	2.0
three	2012	Mumbai	10.2	0.0
four	2010	Hyderabad	5.2	9.0
five	2011	Hyderabad	5.3	-0.4
six	2012	Hyderabad	5.5	7.0

Let's assign a series to it as shown here:

```
val = pd.Series([-1.4, 1.5, -1.3], index=['two', 'four', 'five'])
df3.GDP = val
print(df3)
```

The following output is the result:

```
       year        city  population  GDP
one    2010      Mumbai        10.0  NaN
two    2011      Mumbai        10.1 -1.4
three  2012      Mumbai        10.2  NaN
four   2010   Hyderabad         5.2  1.5
five   2011   Hyderabad         5.3 -1.3
six    2012   Hyderabad         5.5  NaN
```

Reading Data Stored in CSV Format

We can read the data stored in a comma-separated value (CSV) format with the method read_csv(). The CSV file could be stored at a remote URL or a location on the disk. Here is an example of reading a CSV file hosted on a URL over the Internet:

```
df = pd.read_csv('https://raw.githubusercontent.com/cs109/2014_
data/master/countries.csv')
df.head(5)
```

The output is as follows:

```
     Country    Region
0    Algeria    AFRICA
1    Angola     AFRICA
2    Benin      AFRICA
3    Botswana   AFRICA
4    Burkina    AFRICA
```

We can read the data stored in a file on the disk into a dataframe in the same way.

Visualizing with Pandas

A pandas dataframe has methods for visualization like Matplotlib. Basically, these methods are wrappers over the methods in Matplotlib. Let's look at how we can use these methods to visualize the data stored in the pandas dataframes.

Let's import the pyplot module of Matplotlib and use the magic command to enable Matplotlib visualization in the notebook as follows:

```
%matplotlib inline
import matplotlib.pyplot as plt
```

The NumPy function randn() generates a NumPy array with a standard normal random distribution. We will use this to create a series and plot it as follows:

```
ts = pd.Series(np.random.randn(5))
ts
```

The output is as follows (it will be different every time you execute the code, as it is randomly generated at the time of execution):

```
0     0.257543
1     1.405170
2     1.290728
3     0.068451
4    -0.923677
dtype: float64
```

This can be visualized as follows:

```
ts.plot()
plt.grid(True)
plt.show()
```

It produces the output shown in Figure 8-1.

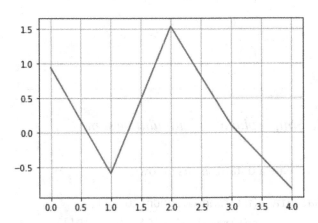

Figure 8-1. *Simple plot*

We can compute the cumulative sum with the function cumsum() and visualize it as follows:

```
ts.cumsum().plot()
plt.grid(True)
plt.show()
```

The output is displayed in Figure 8-2.

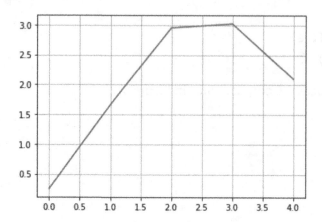

Figure 8-2. *Simple plot of the cumulative sum*

Now let's create a dataframe as follows:

```
df1 = pd.DataFrame(np.random.randn(10, 4),
                   columns=['A', 'B', 'C', 'D'])
print(df1)
```

The following output is the result:

```
          A         B         C         D
0   0.474219  1.821673 -0.296638 -0.566934
1   1.820044  2.199264  2.196097  0.203744
2   0.086325 -1.056730  0.937690 -1.283733
3   0.087798  1.145512 -0.407545  0.747684
4  -0.179241  0.290476  1.823487 -0.059593
5   1.964211 -0.525957  1.615896  0.046840
6  -0.463331  0.032999  1.130027  1.151667
7   1.805051 -0.338121 -0.397105  0.487373
8  -1.212102 -0.610992  0.258653 -1.885551
9  -1.052613  1.624191  0.529037  1.081536
```

We can visualize this with vertical bar graphs as follows:

```
df1.plot.bar()
plt.grid(True)
plt.show()
```

The output is displayed in Figure 8-3.

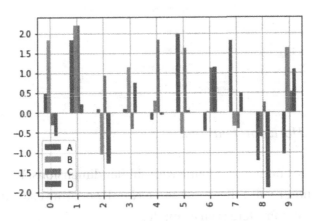

Figure 8-3. *Vertical bar plot*

You can even use horizontal bar graphs as follows:

```
df1.plot.barh()
plt.grid(True)
plt.show()
```

Figure 8-4 displays the output.

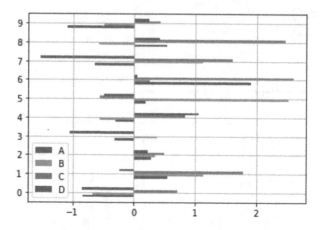

Figure 8-4. *Horizontal bar plot*

Let's create another dataframe with similar dimensions. We will use the function rand() that generates a NumPy ndarray using uniform normal distribution. Here is an example:

```
df2 = pd.DataFrame(np.random.rand(10, 4), columns=['A', 'B',
'C', 'D'])
print(df2)
```

The output is shown here:

```
          A         B         C         D
0  0.416596  0.725513  0.707631  0.286249
1  0.166804  0.370956  0.680678  0.938911
2  0.330940  0.426264  0.667221  0.741184
3  0.879112  0.409153  0.460051  0.968562
4  0.248149  0.021732  0.072309  0.186000
5  0.666609  0.692510  0.574111  0.519540
6  0.178994  0.437883  0.036931  0.063519
7  0.057269  0.079832  0.025361  0.150671
```

```
8   0.099039   0.886589   0.358671   0.431321
9   0.395520   0.262707   0.291207   0.763712
```

We can create stacked vertical bar graphs as follows:

```
df2.plot.bar(stacked=True)
plt.grid(True)
plt.show()
```

That produces the output shown in Figure 8-5.

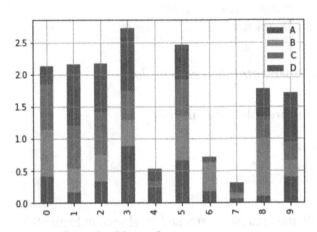

Figure 8-5. *Vertical stacked bar plot*

Similarly, we can produce horizontal stacked bar plots as follows:

```
df2.plot.barh(stacked=True)
plt.grid(True)
plt.show()
```

The output is displayed in Figure 8-6.

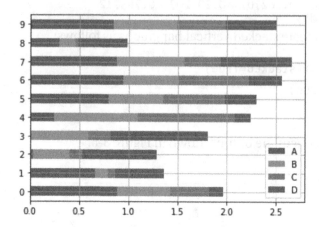

Figure 8-6. *Horizontal stacked bar plot*

To create an area plot, use this code:

```
df2.plot.area()
plt.grid(True)
plt.show()
```

By default, the area plot is stacked, as shown in Figure 8-7.

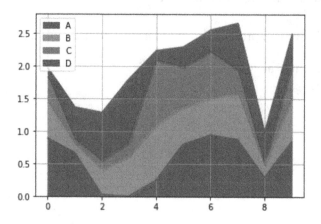

Figure 8-7. *Stacked area plot*

You can create an unstacked overlapping area plot as follows:

```
df2.plot.area(stacked=False)
plt.grid(True)
plt.show()
```

That produces the output shown in Figure 8-8.

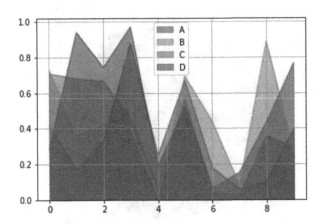

Figure 8-8. *Overlapping area plot*

Next let's demonstrate a pie chart. Create a simple dataframe as follows:

```
df3 = pd.DataFrame(np.random.rand(4), index=['A', 'B', 'C',
'D'])
print(df3)
```

The following is the output:

```
           0
A   0.292772
B   0.569819
C   0.835805
D   0.479885
```

Use this code to create the pie chart:

```
df3.eplot.pie(subplots=True)
plt.show()
```

The result is shown in Figure 8-9.

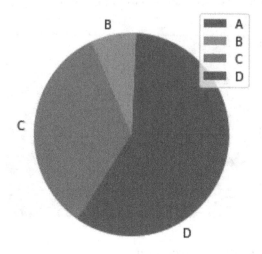

Figure 8-9. *Pie chart*

Summary

This chapter explored the basics of the data science library of SciPy, pandas. You learned the basics of creation and operations on the fundamental pandas data structures, series and dataframes. You also learned the basics of visualizing dataframe data and how to read the data from a CSV file.

All these concepts will be very useful to in completing the exercise in the next chapter. The next chapter concludes our data visualization journey by working with data related to the ongoing COVID-19 pandemic. It provides an interesting real-life case study.

CHAPTER 9

Working with COVID-19 Data

Chapter 8 covered the basics of the data science library of SciPy, pandas. You learned the basics of the series and dataframe data structures and how to visualize the data in the dataframes and series.

This chapter is the culmination of all the knowledge you have gained in the earlier chapters. In this chapter, we are going to retrieve real-life data and visualize it. At the conclusion of this chapter, you should be comfortable with visualizations of a real-life data set.

The COVID-19 Pandemic and the Data Set

At the time of writing of this book, the world is facing an unprecedented natural calamity, a pandemic (an infectious disease spreading across continents) caused by the severe acute respiratory syndrome coronavirus 2 (SARS-CoV-2) and the resulting disease known as COVID-19. This virus comes from the same family of viruses (Coronaviruses) that cause nonlethal diseases like the common cold and more lethal diseases like SARS and MERS. These viruses cause infections of the respiratory tract in mammals and humans and can be lethal if not treated in a timely manner.

© Ashwin Pajankar 2021
A. Pajankar, *Practical Python Data Visualization*,
https://doi.org/10.1007/978-1-4842-6455-3_9

Data Sources for COVID-19 Data

Many organizations are keeping track of COVID-19 cases worldwide and updating the data on their website and web services periodically. The most prominent are Johns Hopkins University (`https://coronavirus.jhu.edu/map.html`) and World-O-Meter (`https://www.worldometers.info/coronavirus/`). These are very reliable sources of data for COVID-19 and they update their statistics very frequently (at least once every 24 hours) so downstream systems get the latest data.

We can retrieve this data using custom libraries in Python. One such library can be found at `https://ahmednafies.github.io/covid/`. It can retrieve the data from both Johns Hopkins University and World-O-Meter. To install it, create a new notebook for this chapter and run the following command in a code cell:

```
!pip3 install covid
```

Next, import the library as follows:

```
from covid import Covid
```

You can fetch the data using this code:

```
covid = Covid()
```

It fetches the data from Johns Hopkins University by default. You can also explicitly mention the data source:

```
covid = Covid(source="john_hopkins")
```

To fetch the data from World-O-Meter, change the source value:

```
covid = Covid(source="worldometers")
```

You can display all the data using the following commad:

```
covid.get_data()
```

This returns a list of dictionaries, as shown in Figure 9-1.

```
In [35]:  # get all data
          covid.get_data()

Out[35]:  [{'country': 'North America',
            'confirmed': 3628797,
            'new_cases': 7809,
            'deaths': 178674,
            'recovered': 1648713,
            'active': 1801410,
            'critical': 18601,
            'new_deaths': 945,
            'total_tests': 0,
            'total_tests_per_million': Decimal('0'),
            'total_cases_per_million': Decimal('0'),
            'total_deaths_per_million': Decimal('0'),
```

Figure 9-1. *COVID-19 data*

We can determine the source of the data as follows:

```
covid.source
```

The output in this case is shown here:

```
'worldometers'
```

You can also retrieve the status by country name as follows:

```
covid.get_status_by_country_name("italy")
```

The result is shown in Figure 9-2.

```
In [37]:  covid.get_status_by_country_name("italy")

Out[37]:  {'country': 'Italy',
           'confirmed': 241956,
           'new_cases': 0,
           'deaths': 34899,
           'recovered': 192815,
           'active': 14242,
           'critical': 70,
           'new_deaths': 0,
           'total_tests': 5703673,
           'total_tests_per_million': Decimal('0'),
           'total_cases_per_million': Decimal('4002'),
           'total_deaths_per_million': Decimal('577'),
           'population': Decimal('60459826')}
```

Figure 9-2. *COVID-19 data by country*

You can retrieve the data by country ID, too (this function is only valid for the Johns Hopkins data source), with this code:

```
covid.get_status_by_country_id(115)
```

To retrieve the list of countries affected by the COVID-19 pandemic, use this syntax:

```
covid.list_countries()
```

It returns the list shown in Figure 9-3.

```
Out[17]:  ['north america',
           'south america',
           'asia',
           'europe',
           'africa',
           'oceania',
           '',
           'world',
           'usa',
           'brazil',
           'india',
           'russia',
           'peru',
           'chile',
           'spain',
```

Figure 9-3. *Countries affected by COVID-19*

The total number of active cases can be obtained as follows:

```
covid.get_total_active_cases()
```

The total number of confirmed cases can be obtained as follows:

```
covid.get_total_confirmed_cases()
```

The total number of recovered cases can be obtained as follows:

```
covid.get_total_recovered()
```

The total number of deaths can be obtained as follows:

```
covid.get_total_deaths()
```

Run those statements and examine the output.

Visualizing the COVID-19 Data

Now you can convert all this data into a pandas dataframe as follows:

```
import pandas as pd
df = pd.DataFrame(covid.get_data())
print(df)
```

The output is shown in Figure 9-4.

```
import pandas as pd
df = pd.DataFrame(covid.get_data())
print(df)
```

	country	confirmed	new_cases	deaths	recovered	active	\
0	North America	3628797	7809	178674	1648713	1801410	
1	South America	2614931	1036	96832	1717350	800749	
2	Asia	2700746	20485	64867	1839062	796817	
3	Europe	2513631	8954	194782	1462217	856632	
4	Africa	511949	779	12026	248751	251172	
..	...	...	...	...	...	...	
218	Caribbean Netherlands	7	0	0	7	0	
219	St. Barth	6	0	0	6	0	
220	Anguilla	3	0	0	3	0	
221	Saint Pierre Miquelon	1	0	0	1	0	

Figure 9-4. *COVID-19 data converted to a dataframe*

Use this code to sort the data:

```
sorted = df.sort_values(by=['confirmed'], ascending=False)
```

This data contains the cumulative data for all the continents and the world, too. We can exclude the data for the world and the continents as follows:

```
excluded = sorted[~sorted.country.isin(['Europe', 'South
America', 'Asia', 'World', 'North America', 'Africa'])]
```

The top 10 countries can be retrieved as follows:

```
top10 = excluded.head(10)
print(top10)
```

The output is shown in Figure 9-5.

```
top10 = excluded.head(10)
print(top10)
```

	country	confirmed	new_cases	deaths	recovered	active	critical
8	USA	3097538	454	133991	1355524	1608023	15371
9	Brazil	1674655	0	66868	1117922	489865	8318
10	India	746506	3025	20684	458618	267204	8944
11	Russia	700792	6562	10667	472511	217614	2300
12	Peru	309278	0	10952	200938	97388	1265
13	Chile	301019	0	6434	268245	26340	2060
14	Spain	299210	0	28392	0	0	617
15	UK	286349	0	44391	0	0	209
16	Mexico	268008	6258	32014	163646	72348	378
17	Iran	248379	2691	12084	209463	26832	3309

Figure 9-5. *Top 10 countries affected by COVID-19*

Now we can extract the data into variables as follows:

```
x = top10.country
y1 = top10.confirmed
y2 = top10.active
y3 = top10.deaths
y4 = top10.recovered
```

Now, we can use the results to visualize. Import Matplotlib and enable plotting on the notebook with this command:

```
%matplotlib inline
import matplotlib.pyplot as plt
```

Create a simple line graph as follows:

```
plt.plot(x, y1)
plt.xticks(rotation=90)
plt.show()
```

The result is shown in Figure 9-6.

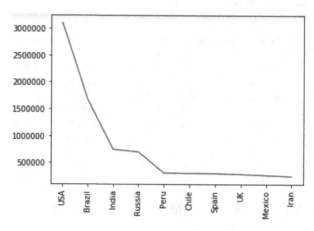

Figure 9-6. *Top 10 countries affected by COVID-19 (line graph)*

We can display the bar graph as follows:

```
plt.bar(x, y1)
plt.xticks(rotation=90)
plt.show()
```

Figure 9-7 displays the result.

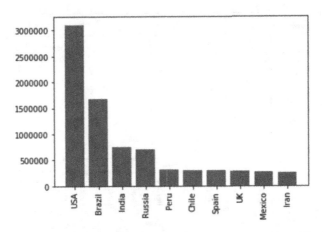

Figure 9-7. *Top 10 countries affected by COVID-19 (bar graph)*

Use this code to create a multiline graph:

```
plt.plot(x, y1, label='Confirmed')
plt.plot(x, y2, label='Active')
plt.plot(x, y3, label='Deaths')
plt.plot(x, y4, label='Recovered')
plt.legend(loc='upper right')
plt.xticks(rotation=90)
plt.show()
```

The output is displayed in Figure 9-8.

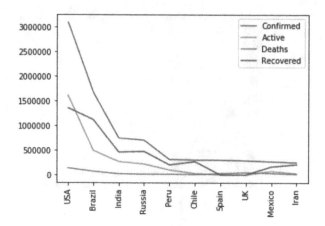

Figure 9-8. *Top 10 countries affected by COVID-19 (multiline graph)*

We can rewrite the preceding example with compact code and better formatting as follows:

```
labels = ['Confirmed', 'Active', 'Deaths', 'Recovered']
plt.plot(x, y1, x, y2, x, y3, x, y4)
plt.legend(labels, loc='upper right')
plt.xticks(rotation=90)
plt.grid()
plt.show()
```

The result is shown in Figure 9-9.

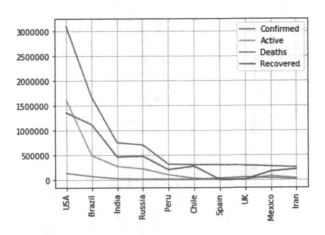

Figure 9-9. Top 10 countries affected by COVID-19 (multiline graph with grids)

We can display the data in vertical multiple bar graphs as follows:

```
df2 = pd.DataFrame([y1, y2, y3, y4])
df2.plot.bar();
plt.legend(x, loc='upper center')
plt.xticks(rotation=90)
plt.grid()
plt.show()
```

Figure 9-10 displays the output.

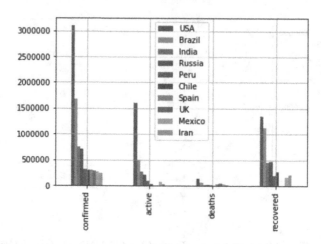

Figure 9-10. *Top 10 countries' COVID-19 statistics (multiple bar graph with grids)*

We can plot the data in vertical stacked bar graphs with the following code:

```
df2.plot.bar(stacked=True);
plt.legend(x, loc='upper center')
plt.xticks(rotation=90)
plt.grid()
plt.show()
```

That produces the output shown in Figure 9-11.

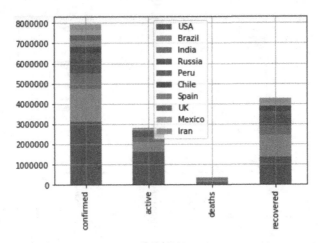

Figure 9-11. *Top 10 countries' COVID-19 statistics (vertical stacked bar graph with grids)*

We can create horizontal bar graphs as follows:

```
df2.plot.barh();
plt.legend(x, loc='upper right')
plt.xticks(rotation=90)
plt.grid()
plt.show()
```

This produces the output shown in Figure 9-12.

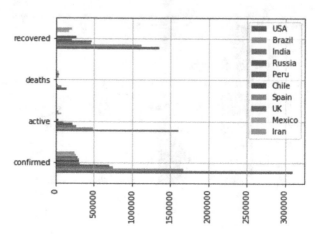

Figure 9-12. *Top 10 countries' COVID-19 statistics (horizontal graph with grid)*

Next, create a stacked horizontal bar visualization with the following code:

```
df2.plot.barh(stacked=True);
plt.legend(x, loc='upper right')
plt.xticks(rotation=90)
plt.grid()
plt.show()
```

The output is shown in Figure 9-13.

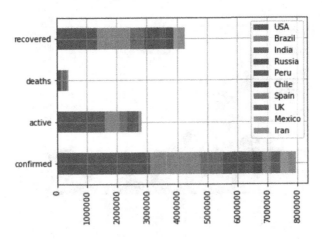

Figure 9-13. *Top 10 countries' COVID-19 statistics (horizontal stacked bar graph with grid)*

We can even use area graphs to visualize this data. By default, the area graph, as we know, is stacked. We can create it as follows:

```
df2.plot.area();
plt.legend(x, loc='upper right')
plt.xticks(rotation=90)
plt.grid()
plt.show()
```

The output is displayed in Figure 9-14.

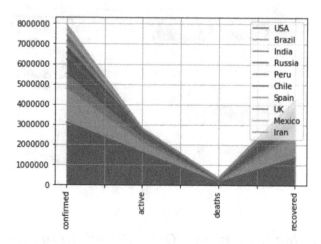

Figure 9-14. *Top 10 countries' COVID-19 statistics (stacked area graph)*

You can even create an overlapping area graph as follows:

```
df2.plot.area(stacked=False);
plt.legend(x, loc='upper right')
plt.xticks(rotation=90)
plt.grid()
plt.show()
```

Figure 9-15 depicts the result.

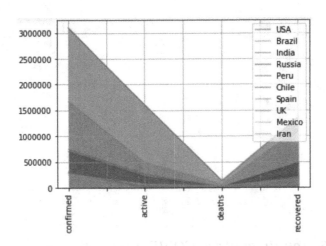

Figure 9-15. *Top 10 countries' COVID-19 statistics (overlapping area graph)*

To create a nice scatter plot where the size of dots is proportional to the magnitude of data, use the following code:

```
factor=0.0001
plt.scatter(x, y1, s=y1*factor);
plt.scatter(x, y2, s=y2*factor);
plt.scatter(x, y3, s=y3*factor);
plt.scatter(x, y4, s=y4*factor);
plt.legend(labels, loc='upper right')
plt.xticks(rotation=90)
plt.grid()
plt.show()
```

The output is shown in Figure 9-16.

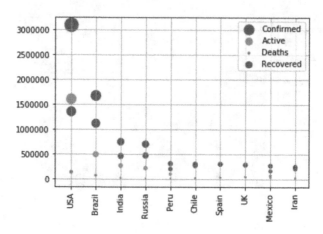

Figure 9-16. *Top 10 countries' COVID-19 statistics (scatter graph)*

Finally, you can create a nice pie chart with the following code:

```
plt.pie(y1, labels=x)
plt.title('Confirmed Cases')
plt.show()
```

The output is shown in Figure 9-17.

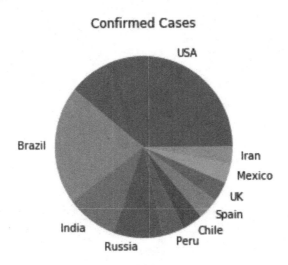

Figure 9-17. Top 10 countries' COVID-19 statistics (pie chart)

Summary

In this chapter, you learned how to retrieve COVID-19 data from various online sources and convert the data to a pandas dataframe. You also saw how to prepare various types of visualizations to represent that COVID-19 data graphically.

This is how we conclude our data visualization journey, working with the real-life data. I hope you enjoyed reading and following the examples in this book as much as I enjoyed writing them. Data visualization is an expansive domain. There are many other Python libraries for data visualization that you can explore, such as ggplot, plotly, and seaborn. These libraries provide advanced data visualization capabilities that might meet your business and scientific visualization requirements.

Index

A, B

Addition operation, 87
arange() function, 60
Arithmetic operations, 85, 100
Assign custom labels, 114

C

Color channels, 89, 91, 92
Comma-separated value (CSV)
    format, 127
Comparison operations, 120
Constructor function, 119
Container, 51
COVID-19, 137
    countries affected, 141
    data by country, 140
    dataframe, 142
    data source, 138–142
    top 10 countries,
        affected, 143
      bar graph, 145
      grids, 147
      horizontal graph, 150
      horizontal stacked bar
        graph, 151
      line graph, 144
      multiline graph, 146

overlapping area graph, 153
    pie chart, 155
    scatter graph, 154
    stacked area graph, 152
    statistics, 148
    vertical stacked bar, 149
    visualizing data, 142
cumsum() function, 129

D, E, F

Dataframes,Pandas, 121–127
Data visualization library
    colors /styles/markers, 73–79
    grid/axes/labels, 68–73
    Matplotlib, 58–63
    multiline plot, 66, 67
    Numpy, 59–63
    single line plot, 64, 66
    types
      bar charts, 41
      customizing line, 38
      line segments, 37
      multiple lines, 39, 40
      vertical columns, 42, 43
Debian, 8
df1.tail() function, 122
Dodecahedral graph, 113

© Ashwin Pajankar 2021
A. Pajankar, *Practical Python Data Visualization*,
https://doi.org/10.1007/978-1-4842-6455-3

Printed in the United States
By Bookmasters